STOKES
Oriole
BOOK

Stokes Field Guides

Stokes Field Guide to Birds: Eastern Region
Stokes Field Guide to Birds: Western Region
Stokes Field Guide to Bird Songs: Eastern Region (CD/cassette)
Stokes Field Guide to Bird Songs: Western Region (CD/cassette)

Stokes Beginner's Guides

Stokes Beginner's Guide to Birds: Eastern Region
Stokes Beginner's Guide to Birds: Western Region

Stokes Backyard Nature Books

Stokes Bird Feeder Book
Stokes Bird Gardening Book
Stokes Birdhouse Book
Stokes Bluebird Book
Stokes Butterfly Book
Stokes Hummingbird Book
Stokes Oriole Book
Stokes Purple Martin Book
Stokes Wildflower Book: East of the Rockies
Stokes Wildflower Book: From the Rockies West

Stokes Nature Guides

Stokes Guide to Amphibians and Reptiles
Stokes Guide to Animal Tracking and Behavior
Stokes Guide to Bird Behavior, Volume 1
Stokes Guide to Bird Behavior, Volume 2
Stokes Guide to Bird Behavior, Volume 3
Stokes Guide to Enjoying Wildflowers
Stokes Guide to Nature in Winter
Stokes Guide to Observing Insect Lives

Other Stokes Books

The Natural History of Wild Shrubs and Vines

STOKES Oriole BOOK

The Complete Guide to Attracting, Identifying, and Enjoying Orioles

DONALD AND LILLIAN STOKES

Little, Brown and Company

Boston   New York   London

First Edition

Library of Congress Cataloging-in-Publication Data
Stokes, Donald W.
    Stokes oriole book : the complete guide to attracting, identifying, and enjoying orioles / by Donald and Lillian Stokes: — 1st ed.
        p.   cm.
    ISBN 0-316-81694-9
    1. Icterus (Birds) Identification. 2. Bird attracting.
I. Stokes, Lillian Q.   II. Title.
QL696.P2475S74 2000
598.8'74 — dc21   99-37698

10 9 8 7 6 5 4 3 2 1

Design and electronic production: Barbara Werden Design

RRD-IN

Printed in the United States of America

Acknowledgments
We would like to thank the following people for assisting us in the research for this book: Jon Dunn, for helping with the identification photos; Alan Poole, for helping us get the accounts of many of the orioles from the superb resource called *Birds of North America*; Sam Droege, for help in getting the abundance maps; Nancy Flood and Barbara Pleasants, for their excellent articles on oriole behavior; Trevor Lloyd-Evans, for his suggestions on molts; and Tim Brush, for his help on southern Texas orioles.

Photograph Acknowledgments
Ron Austing: 18 (fig. 23), 40, 86
Cliff Beittel: 17 (fig. 19)
Steve Bentsen: 22 (fig. 36), 26 (fig. 44), 67, 68, 69
Herbert Clarke: 22 (fig.31), 25 (fig.40), 65, 91
Richard Day/Daybreak Imagery: 12 (fig. 5), 52, 53, 54
Larry Ditto: 76 top
Roger Eriksson: 26 (fig. 43), 42
James R. Gallagher/Sea and Sage Audubon: 15 (fig. 13), 16 (fig. 17), 21 (figs. 29, 30), 22 (fig. 32), 24 (fig. 38), 48, 82, 83
Susan Gallagher/Sea and Sage Audubon: 50
B. B. Hall/Cornell Laboratory of Ornithology, 27 (fig. 47), 92
Robert McCaw: 12 (fig. 2), 13 (fig. 8), 14 (fig. 10), 19 (fig. 26), 36, 41
Maslowski Photo: 18 (fig. 22)
Charles W. Melton: 15 (fig. 15), 24 (fig. 39), 90
Anthony Mercieca: 16 (fig. 16), 20 (fig. 27), 23 (fig. 35), 25 (fig. 41), 26 (fig. 45), 38, 76 bottom
Nature Products Inc.: 37
Opus Inc.: 39
Dan Panetti: 43
Marie Read: 70
Jim Roetzel: 49, 57, 58, 61, 74
Brian Small: 7, 12 (fig. 4), 13 (figs. 6, 7), 17 (fig. 20), 19 (fig. 25), 23 (figs. 34, 36), 25 (fig. 42), 27 (fig. 46), 56, 62, 72, 77, 79, 80, 81, 84, 85, 87, 89, 93, 95
Hugh Smith Jr.: 14 (fig. 12), 15 (fig. 14), 16 (fig. 18), 46
John Snyder: 24 (fig. 37), 88
Sherm Spoelstra: 20 (fig. 28), 44, 51, 78
Tom Vezo: 1, 12 (fig. 3), 13 (fig. 9), 14 (fig. 11), 18 (fig. 21), 19 (fig. 24), 33, 34, 45, 60, 71, 73

Contents

The Joy of Orioles

Special American Birds

Orioles are one of America's favorite backyard birds. Their strikingly beautiful black and orange or yellow plumage, their whistled spring songs that ring out from the treetops, their amazing suspended nests that are an architectural wonder of the avian world, and their endearing habit of choosing our backyards as their summer homes all make them a special bird that is close to our hearts.

Add to this their incredible journey from our temperate zone to the tropics and back each year and you begin to realize what a wonderful symbol orioles are for the rhythms of life on the American continents.

There are a total of twenty-four species of orioles in the world, and they all live in North or South America. Orioles are medium-sized birds with relatively long bills and long tails, and they tend to live in habitats where there are shrubs and trees from tropical to semiarid regions. They are often found along rivers or the edges of woods.

Orioles are closely related to blackbirds, grackles, meadowlarks, and cowbirds. Together, these groups, and several others, make up the family of birds collectively called blackbirds; the scientific name is Icteridae. Icteridae comes from the Greek word for "yellow," referring to the yellow plumage of many members of this family.

In the United States there are ten species of orioles that can be seen, eight of them regularly. Of these, five are highly migratory, moving between breeding and wintering grounds each year. The rest are generally year-round residents within their ranges.

All of our orioles show variations on the theme of black with yellow or orange plumage. In the adult males, tails and wings are mostly black and the head is either all black or black on just the face and throat.

The only exception is the adult male Bullock's Oriole, which has a black cap, black eyeline, and black throat. Most of the adult females have sooty wings, dusky yellow or orange tails, and more limited black on the head and throat.

Interestingly, the five species that are migratory are also strongly **dimorphic,** meaning that adult males and females look very different. The resident species are primarily **monomorphic** — adult males and females look alike. One possible reason for this pattern is that migratory birds need to settle and find mates quickly when they arrive on their breeding grounds, and having the sexes look different facilitates rapid pairing. Birds that are year-round residents have more time to set up territories and find mates, or they may simply stay together as pairs all year, making quick recognition less important.

Your Complete Oriole Handbook

In this book we have created the first complete guide to North American orioles. We hope that it will increase your enjoyment of all aspects of these fascinating birds.

The first section, "An Introduction to Orioles," focuses on the identification and ranges of orioles. Included here is a field guide offering the most complete photographic collection of oriole plumages that has ever been assembled. Oriole identification can be complex, and we have tried to simplify the process and make it accessible to everyone. We also include special maps that indicate the relative abundance of the major species and we discuss their population trends. Finally, we discuss oriole conservation and issues facing these birds in the coming decades.

In the second section, "Attracting Orioles," we explore all of the ways you can attract orioles to your yard. There are many things that you can do, such as put up a variety of feeders, offer nesting material,

A male Baltimore Oriole looking for insects.

plant wild fruits, plant orioles' favorite nesting trees, and create habitats in which orioles will choose to breed. All of these actions will greatly increase your chances of getting orioles to visit and even nest in your backyard.

The third section of the book, "Enjoying Oriole Behavior," is designed to help you appreciate and understand the orioles you have attracted. Here we describe the complete life histories of all the major species in the United States and Canada. We also have a special chapter detailing a day in the life of a Baltimore Oriole, giving you a close-up look into the world of a parent bird raising young.

Finally, we have included a list of resources from a variety of media — magazines, books, videos, and the web — that will enable you to learn more on your own.

A Bird's-eye View

Over the years, we have written many books on attracting birds and other wildlife to your backyard, and with each one we gain a deeper appreciation for life.

Of all the ways to be involved with birds, we find attracting them to be one of the most absorbing and rewarding. In order to attract a bird species, you have to know how they see the world. You need to know the size of their territories, the habitats where they feed, the foods they eat, the places they nest, the materials with which they build their nest, and their changing social arrangements as they pass in and out of the breeding season. You must know their needs during each of the seasons, their arrival and departure schedule, and what they consider shelter.

Trying to attract a bird is a refreshing and challenging exercise. It forces you, if only for a moment, to move beyond our limited human perspective and get a brief glimpse of the world from the point of view of another species with which we share the planet.

We wish you the best of luck in attracting orioles. If you succeed, then you will know you have offered something they need in their lives. You will have increased the value of your yard in orioles' lives, and in so doing, you will have undoubtedly increased its richness for other living things as well.

When you do this, you increase the quality of life for yourself, your family, and everyone else with whom you share your property.

Yours in attracting birds,
Lillian and Don Stokes

Identifying North American Orioles

How Many and Where?

There are eight species of orioles seen regularly in North America north of Mexico. Of these, only five species have large ranges that cover several states. They are the Baltimore and Orchard Orioles, which live primarily in eastern and central portions of the country; the Bullock's Oriole, which lives throughout the West; and the Scott's and Hooded Orioles, which live in the Southwest and California.

The other three species have very limited ranges. The Altamira and Audubon's Orioles live only in the southern tip of Texas, and the Spot-breasted Oriole lives on the east coast of Florida.

Two Mexican species of orioles are seen irregularly in the southern United States. These are the Streak-backed Oriole, which can sometimes be seen in southeast Arizona and rarely in California, and the Black-vented Oriole, which has been sighted in southern Texas and Arizona. The Black-vented is so rare in the United States that we have not included it in this guide.

Plumage Phases in Orioles

Feathers are a bird's only protection from the elements, and they do not last forever. Because plumage wears out, birds periodically molt some or all of their feathers and grow new ones. When you try to identify a bird, it is important to be aware of this, because molting can cause birds to have different plumages at various ages and seasons. This is particularly true with orioles. This section explains how molts occur in orioles and is essential background for the identification information that follows.

All orioles are featherless when they first hatch, but they quickly grow a set of downy feathers. These

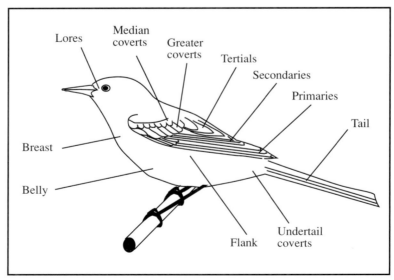

Names of Oriole Feathers

Plumages, Molts, and Their Timings in North American Orioles

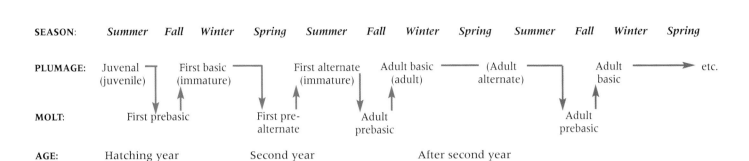

are soon molted and replaced by a full set of feathers just before the bird leaves the nest; this first full set of feathers is called the **juvenal plumage.**

These feathers are kept until late summer and fall, when the bird undergoes what is known as the **first prebasic molt**. The bird may molt just some body feathers, or it may molt all of its body feathers and some wing and tail feathers as well. What grows in afterward is called the **first basic plumage**.

In the next spring, many orioles go through another variable molt, which again may include just some body feathers, or as much as all body feathers and some wing and tail feathers. This is called the **first prealternate molt**. The new plumage is what we see in summer and is called the **first alternate plumage**.

In late summer and fall, orioles undergo a complete molt of all body and flight feathers. This is the **adult prebasic molt**, and the new plumage is called the **adult basic plumage**. In summer this same plumage is referred to as **adult alternate plumage** (in some birds it is different; in adult orioles it is the same plumage, though it may show some wear).

From then on in their lives, adult orioles have only one molt per year, the prebasic molt in fall. In some cases, you may see light edges on the birds' body feathers right after the fall molt, especially on the dark areas of males, but these wear off by the fol-

lowing summer. For most adult orioles (except some of the females), plumage patterns and colors do not change for the rest of their lives.

There are two other common ways of referring to plumage. One system divides plumages into three stages. Birds in juvenal plumage are called **juveniles**. Birds in first basic and first alternate plumage are called **immatures**. Birds in adult basic or adult alternate plumage are called **adults**.

The other system is based on the calendar year — January 1 to December 31 — and more properly refers to the age of a bird. A bird in its first calendar year is called a **hatching-year bird** (HY). A bird in its second calendar year is called a **second-year bird** (SY). A bird in its third calendar year is called an **after-second-year bird** (ASY) or a **third-year bird** (TY).

Each system has its advantages, and we will be using all three in the following descriptions.

Some General Notes About Color

Several generalizations can be made about the appearance of our orioles. Almost all have large amounts of orange, yellow, or greenish yellow on their bodies. The wings are black in adult males and sooty brown in females and most immatures. The wings usually have some white on the median and greater coverts that creates what are called wing-bars; there is also usually white on the edges of the flight feathers called secondaries and primaries (see diagram). In females and most immatures, the tail is usually a dusky shade of the color of the body; in adult males it is mostly black.

Adult male orioles are quite distinct, and their bold patterns of colors make them easy to identify. The females and immature males are more difficult to tell apart. Not only do adult females and immatures of a particular species tend to resemble each other, they also tend to look like the females and/or immatures of other oriole species.

Clues to Identifying Females and Immature Males

To identify females and similar-looking immatures, you need to take note of many different features of their appearance. Here is a checklist of things to observe as you try to identify them. Look first at the shape of the bird. Notice its size; the shape, length, and slenderness or thickness of the bill; and whether the bill is straight or slightly downcurved. Also look at the tail to see how long it is in relation to the body and whether the feathers are all roughly the same length, making it squarish at the tip, or whether the outer feathers are noticeably shorter, making the tip rounded or graduated.

After looking at the shape, look at the overall color of the bird — is it yellow, orangish, or greenish? Is it evenly colored or brighter in some areas? And finally look at the back; is it fairly uniform and one color, or is it mottled or streaked with black?

Also, use the range maps to help narrow down the identification possibilities during the breeding season, when fewer species intermingle. During spring and fall migration, especially in southern Texas, there can be many more species in the area than usual, and identification is more challenging. Some species wander far during migration, and occasionally East Coast orioles show up along the West Coast and vice versa. In many cases, these vagrants are misidentified, because most field guides do not include enough information to help people distinguish among females and immatures of several species.

Field Guide to North American Orioles

The following pages offer species descriptions and photographs of nine species of orioles found in North America. Each species account begins with a general description of the size and shape of that species, followed by a detailed description of its color patterns. The extended captions accompanying the identification pictures provide important additional identification tips. When known, the month the photograph was taken is given, as this can be an important factor in making an identification. A map shows the North American range for each species (yellow=summer range, blue=winter range, green=year-round range).

Baltimore Oriole

The Baltimore Oriole is a medium-sized oriole with a medium-length straight bill and a short square tail. The breast and undertail coverts are orange.

There is more variability in the plumage of Baltimore Orioles than in any of our other species, especially in SY males and females of all ages. This is probably due to the variable amount of molt they undergo in their first prebasic and first prealternate molts. Also, some ASY males are brighter orange than others; whether this is age related is not known.

An interesting complication in Baltimore Oriole identification is that the female's plumage changes as she gets older. In her HY, SY, and TY she may have no black feathers on her head. However, in her third year she usually starts to get a mottled black hood and back, which may become more solid with age, until she looks much like an adult male.

Confusing matters further, the male's head is mottled to varying degrees during his SY, making him look like some ASY females. The key to distinguishing SY males and ASY females is to look first at feathers on the bird's wings, to determine its age, and then to look at the amount of black on its head, wings, and tail, to determine its sex.

Figure 1. This is a SY female in first alternate plumage. Photo taken in April–May. The short, dashlike lower wingbar (which occurs in most SY individuals) and the ragged worn edges of the secondaries and primaries indicate that this is a SY bird. The dusky head, grayish-brown unmarked back, orange breast, and lack of black on the head show that it is a female.

Fig. 1. Baltimore Oriole, SY female

Fig. 2. Baltimore Oriole, SY female

Figure 2. This is a SY female in first alternate plumage. The fact that just some of the greater coverts are molted and have white tips and the rest of the wing feathers are worn and brown shows that this is a SY bird. The new coverts are a sooty color, suggesting this is a female; they would be jet-black in the male.

Fig. 3. Baltimore Oriole, ASY female

Figure 3. This is an ASY female in adult alternate plumage. Photo taken in May. The complete lower wingbar, the uniformly sooty wing feathers, and the white edges to the primaries and secondaries show that this is an ASY bird. The lack of black mottling on the head and back, and the sooty, rather than black, wing show that this is a female.

Fig. 4. Baltimore Oriole, ASY female

Figure 4. This is an ASY female in adult alternate plumage. The complete lower wingbar, the uniformly sooty wing feathers, and the white edges to the primaries and secondaries show that this is an ASY bird. The black mottling on the head and back, the sooty, rather than black, wing, and the dusky orange tail show that this is a female.

Fig. 5. Baltimore Oriole, ASY female

Figure 5. This is another example of an ASY female in adult alternate plumage. The bird's almost all black head makes it look much like a SY or even ASY male. The complete lower wingbar, the uniformly dark brown wing feathers, and the white edges to the primaries and secondaries show that it is an ASY bird. The absence of pure black on the head, back, wings, and tail indicates that it is actually a female.

Fig. 6. Baltimore Oriole, SY male

Figure 6. This is a SY male in first alternate plumage. The incomplete lower wingbar, the contrast between the newer black greater coverts and the older brown coverts, and the wear and lack of white on the edges of the primaries and secondaries show this is a SY bird. The mottling on the head and back, the black of the new greater coverts, and the black central tail feathers show that this is a male.

Fig. 7. Baltimore Oriole, SY male

Figure 7. This is a SY male in first alternate plumage. The extremely worn feathers on the wing and tail show that this is a SY bird. The jet-black feathers on the head and back show that this is a male.

Fig. 8. Baltimore Oriole, SY male

Figure 8. This is a SY male in first alternate plumage. The short lower wingbar, the lack of white edges on the primaries and secondaries, the contrasting white on the edges of the tertials, and the contrast between the older brown and newer black feathers on the wing show that this is a SY bird. The black on the head, back, and central tail feathers and the new black wing feathers show that it is a male.

Fig. 9. Baltimore Oriole, SY male

Figure 9. This is a SY male in first alternate plumage. Photo taken in May. The short lower wingbar, the lack of white edges on the primaries and secondaries, and the contrasting white on one tertial show that this is a SY bird. It is a SY male because it has a completely black head and the new feathers on its greater coverts are black. Interestingly, although the body feathers are so advanced, the central tail feathers are still dusky orange and have not been molted (they will be black).

Fig. 10. Baltimore Oriole, SY male

Fig. 11. Baltimore Oriole, ASY male

Figure 10. This is a SY male in first alternate plumage. The short lower wingbar, worn wing feathers, and contrast in color between the brown older feathers and black newer ones show that this is a SY bird. The black head and newer feathers on the wing show that this is a male. Note that the central tail feathers have been molted into the adult black.

Figure 11. This is an ASY male in adult alternate plumage. The completely black wing and the strong white edges on the primaries and secondaries show that this is an adult. The black head and black central tail feathers show that this is a male.

Bullock's Oriole

A medium-sized oriole with a medium-length straight bill and a relatively square tail. Color on the breast varies from yellow to orange.

The adult male Bullock's Oriole is distinctive. The SY males and SY and ASY females are hard to distin-guish. Also, there can be some confusion in distin-guishing Bullock's and Baltimore Orioles in their HY and SY plumages, since the two species are similar in size and shape, their ranges overlap in the Midwest, and both may wander during migration. In general, look for extensive gray on the belly and breast of the Bullock's and look for the suggestion of an eyeline. The Baltimore is usually yellow to orange on the belly and breast and has no eyeline. If a Baltimore has gray on the body, it is usually limited to the lower belly, right around the area of the legs.

Fig. 12. Bullock's Oriole, juvenile

Figure 12. This is a juvenal plumage bird. Photo taken in July. The perfect quality of all the feathers and the pink lower bill show that this is a juvenile. At this stage, male and female are similar.

Fig. 13. Bullock's Oriole, SY female

Figure 13. This is a SY female in first alternate plumage. Photo taken in May. The worn edges of the secondaries and primaries indicate a SY bird. The very limited yellow on the face, the lack of black on the throat or face, and the extensive gray over the body indicate a female.

Fig. 14. Bullock's Oriole, SY female

Figure 14. This is another SY female in first alternate plumage. Photo taken in June. The extremely worn wing feathers indicate that this is a SY bird. The limited yellow and lack of black on the face indicate a female. Note the extensive gray on the bodies of the birds in Figures 13 and 14 and the lack of yellow on the undertail coverts; these points help distinguish Bullock's from Baltimore Orioles, in which undertail coverts are always orange and any gray on the belly is limited to the area around the legs.

Fig. 15. Bullock's Oriole, ASY female

Figure 15. This is an ASY female in adult alternate plumage. Because the wing feathers all have white edges, there is more extensive orangish yellow on the head, and there is no black on the face or throat, this is probably an ASY female. This is still an extensively gray bird compared to a young male or female Baltimore Oriole and it is just barely orange; you can also see a suggestion of a gray eyeline typical of female and SY Bullock's Orioles.

Fig. 16. Bullock's Oriole, **ASY female**

Figure 16. This is another ASY female in adult alternate plumage. This bird is very similar to the one in Figure 15 except that a white chin is visible, which further distinguishes it from a SY male Bullock's and all Baltimores.

Fig. 17. Bullock's Oriole, **ASY female**

Figure 17. This is an ASY female in adult alternate plumage. Photo taken in April. The uniformly fresh wing feathers help indicate that this is an adult. It has black on the throat but in a narrow and limited area; note also that the lores are charcoal and not black. These two features indicate that this is an adult female, which can have black on the throat. Compare with Figure 18.

Fig. 18. Bullock's Oriole, **SY male**

Figure 18. This is a SY male in first alternate plumage. Photo taken in April. The black on the chin, the black lores, and the black on the forehead all indicate a SY male. This is similar to Figure 17 except that this bird has more wear on the feathers, suggesting a SY bird, and it has black on the lores and forehead.

Figure 19. This is an ASY male in adult basic plumage. Note the distinctive white wing patch and black line through the eye. The ASY male has the most orange of all the ages and sexes of Bullock's Orioles.

Fig. 19. Bullock's Oriole, ASY male

Orchard Oriole

A small oriole with a short, moderately downcurved bill and a short square tail.

Orchard Orioles are the smallest of our orioles. Their overall size, along with their short tail and short downcurved bill, will help you identify them. Males are distinctive in their second year and after because of the chestnut feathers in their plumage.

Here again, females are the ones most likely to be confused with other orioles. The adult female Orchard Oriole is uniformly greenish yellow on her body except for her back, which is brownish gray. The body color, its uniformity, and the lack of other markings are clues to her identity. Another clue is the size of her head, which is relatively large in proportion to her body. The female Hooded Oriole, with which the Orchard Oriole can be confused, has a smaller head in relation to her larger body.

Figure 20. Though it is not always possible to determine the age of females in the field, this is probably a SY female in first alternate plumage. This bird's pale grayish wings with worn feather edges, pale yellow head and belly, and slightly dusky hood suggest a SY female. A SY male would have black on his face.

Fig. 20. Orchard Oriole, SY female (?)

Fig. 21. Orchard Oriole, ASY female

Figure 21. This is an ASY female in adult alternate plumage. Photo taken in May. The overall bright greenish-yellow color of this bird's body and the strong white edges on the wing feathers suggest an ASY bird. The absence of black on the face indicates that it is a female.

Fig. 22. Orchard Oriole, ASY female

Figure 22. This is another ASY female in adult alternate plumage. Similar to Figure 21. Note the lack of any variation in the pattern of the body; there is one uniform color from the head through the underbody to the undertail coverts and even the tail. This is characteristic of ASY female Orchard Orioles.

Fig. 23. Orchard Oriole, ASY female

Figure 23. This is an ASY female in adult alternate plumage. Some adult female Orchard Orioles, probably in their third year or later, acquire a few chestnut or black feathers in their plumage. This female is getting chestnut feathers in her lesser and median coverts and is probably three or more years old.

Fig. 24. Orchard Oriole, SY male

Figure 24. This is a SY male in first alternate plumage. Photo taken in May. This bird is recognized as male because of its uniformly greenish-yellow body and the black on its face and throat. These SY males typically show some other black and/or chestnut feathers on their bodies, often the head, breast, and/or undertail coverts. This bird has extensive chestnut on its breast.

Fig. 25. Orchard Oriole, SY male

Figure 25. This is another SY male in first alternate plumage. This is similar to Figure 24 and shows another example of where the black and chestnut feathers can occur. On this bird, chestnut feathers appear on the cheek, breast, and undertail coverts, while flecks of black are all over its head.

Fig. 26. Orchard Oriole, ASY male

Figure 26. This is an ASY male in adult basic plumage. This adult male has the typical black and chestnut feathers distinctive of adult male Orchard Orioles. In winter, there are yellowish-green tips to the feathers, but these wear off in spring, revealing just pure chestnut and black beneath.

Hooded Oriole

A medium-sized oriole (although its size varies with geographical location) with a slender downcurved bill and a long rounded tail (the outer tail feathers are much shorter than the central ones).

The Hooded Oriole adult male is distinctive, with a black face and throat and yellow to orange body. The female is similar to female Orchard and Bullock's Orioles in coloration, but is larger, has a longer tail, and unlike Bullock's has a downcurved bill (Bullock's has a straight bill).

One key factor distinguishing these three adult females from one another is coloration. While the female Bullock's always has extensive pure gray on the belly and the female Orchard is uniformly colored on the body, the Hooded female is somewhere in between. It is not uniformly colored, having a paler belly than head and undertail; this paler area is not the pure gray color of the Bullock's, but has a yellow wash like the Orchard Oriole. Keeping these color patterns in mind while noting differences in size and shape can help you distinguish these three females.

The SY males of these three species are also similar, in that they have yellow to orangish bodies and limited black on the face and throat. The Orchard Oriole is the only one of the three to show some chestnut on the body. The Bullock's is the only one with a straight bill. And the Hooded has the longest tail.

Fig. 27. Hooded Oriole, juvenile

Figure 27. This is a juvenal plumage bird. Photo taken in July. The perfect condition of all the feathers and the pink lower bill show that this is a juvenile.

Fig. 28. Hooded Oriole, ASY female (?)

Figure 28. This is probably an ASY female in adult alternate plumage. Photo taken in April. Note that the whole body is washed with color, richer on the head and undertail coverts than on the belly; this is typical of female Hooded Orioles. It is not always possible to determine the age of female Hooded Orioles in the field. Given the lack of wear on the wings, this is probably an adult.

Fig. 29. Hooded Oriole, ASY female (?)

Figure 29. This is probably another ASY female in adult alternate plumage. Photo taken in March. This is a good example of the proportions of the Hooded Oriole and its long tail. This female has richer yellow on the head than the bird in Figure 28.

Fig. 30. Hooded Oriole, SY male

Figure 30. This is a SY male in first alternate plumage. Photo taken in April. Note the extensive black on the throat and that the belly is a paler orange than the head. The SY male Bullock's has a gray belly, limited black on the throat, black lores, and the suggestion of an eyeline; the SY male Orchard Oriole has black on the face and throat and occasional chestnut feathers on the body.

Fig. 31. Hooded Oriole, ASY male

Figure 31. This is an ASY male in adult basic plumage. The adult male Hooded Oriole does not have a black hood, as you might expect from the name, but a yellow to orange hood. Note also his large white upper wingbar created by the median coverts. This male has yellow tips to his back feathers, showing that he is still in adult basic plumage. As these wear off, he is considered to be in adult alternate plumage.

Fig. 32. Hooded Oriole, ASY male

Figure 32. This is an ASY male in adult alternate plumage. Photo taken in June. Note that in this male the white edges of the tertials and greater coverts, so obvious on the bird in Figure 30, have all worn off. Even the wingbar looks a little ragged. Within a month he will start his complete prebasic molt and get fresh feathers.

Fig. 33. Hooded Oriole, ASY male

Figure 33. This is an ASY male in adult alternate plumage. This male has more extensive black on the face than the male in Figure 32 and is orange rather than yellow. These characteristics are typical of the subspecies in Texas. The yellow subspecies of Hooded Orioles breeds farther to the west, from New Mexico to California.

Scott's Oriole

A large oriole with a relatively short tail and relatively long straight bill.

Females and SY male Scott's Orioles are markedly olive green on the head, breast, and back and a more yellow-olive on the underbody. This coloration, along with their mottled back and larger size, makes them easy to identify as Scott's Orioles. However, because females and SY males also have varying amounts of black on their heads, it remains difficult to determine age and sex of all but adult males.

Fig. 34. Scott's Oriole, ASY female (?)

Figure 34. This is probably an ASY female in adult alternate plumage, but it could be a SY female in first alternate plumage. It is hard to tell the age of this bird and would certainly be difficult in the field. It is a female because of the lack of black on the face.

Fig. 35. Scott's Oriole, ASY female (?)

Figure 35. This is probably an ASY female in adult alternate plumage. The wing feathers of this bird are all fresher than those of an immature bird would be. This is an example of a female with just a little black on the face.

Fig. 36. Scott's Oriole, ASY female (?)

Figure 36. This is probably an ASY female in adult alternate plumage. As with the bird in Figure 35, the wing freshness suggests an adult, so this is an example of a female with a great deal of black on her face.

Fig. 37. Scott's Oriole, SY male

Figure 37. This is a SY male in first alternate plumage. Photo taken in April. The short, dashlike lower wingbar and the lack of white on the edges of the primaries and secondaries suggest that this is a SY bird. The extensive black on the throat suggests that it is male. In general, females in their second year have little or no black on the throat.

Fig. 38. Scott's Oriole, SY male

Figure 38. This is a SY male in first alternate plumage. Photo taken in April. The contrast between the older brown and newer black feathers in the wing shows that this is a SY bird. The extensive black on the body shows that it is a male.

Fig. 39. Scott's Oriole, ASY male

Figure 39. This is an ASY male in adult alternate plumage. This is the distinctive adult male plumage. The black hood and back and the yellow going halfway down the tail feathers help distinguish it from the similar Audubon's Oriole.

Altamira Oriole

The Altamira Oriole is a large oriole with a short thick bill and a long black tail. The sexes are alike.

In general, Altamira Orioles can be seen only in extreme southern Texas, where there are 125 breeding pairs. This oriole's range is largely Mexican, with its northernmost point just over the border into the United States. It is distinctive in that it's our largest oriole, and it has a very short, thick-based bill and bright orange-and-black plumage. It has black from the base of the bill to the eye and down the throat. The sexes look alike. SY birds look different from adults, as they are pale orange and have a dusky orange back and sooty gray wings. They are less commonly seen than the adults.

Fig. 40. Altamira Oriole, SY bird

Figure 40. This is a SY bird in first alternate plumage. Note the paler orange body, the dusky orange back and tail, and the sooty gray wings — all signs of the SY Altamira Oriole.

Fig. 41. Altamira Oriole, ASY bird

Figure 41. This is an ASY bird in adult alternate plumage. Note the black mask, the white triangle on the wing at the base of the primaries, and the short thick bill.

Fig. 42. Altamira Oriole, ASY bird

Figure 42. This is an ASY bird in adult alternate plumage. This view of the back of an Altamira Oriole clearly shows the black back and the bright orange rump.

Audubon's Oriole

This is a large oriole with a medium-sized, thick straight bill and a long rounded tail.

The range of the Audubon's Oriole is limited, and in the United States birds are seen almost exclusively in southern Texas. The Audubon's Oriole is similar to the adult male Scott's Oriole in that it is yellowish with a black hood. It differs in having an all-yellow back and an all-black undertail. The sexes look alike.

Fig. 43. Audubon's Oriole, SY bird (?)

Fig. 44. Audubon's Oriole, ASY bird

Figure 43. This is probably a SY bird in first basic plumage. Photo taken in January. Signs of this being a SY bird are the mixed greenish-yellow and black crown and the greenish edges to the outer tail feathers. Some SY birds show shortened lower wing-bars like those seen in Baltimore Orioles. This individual does not seem to have them.

Figure 44. This is an ASY bird in adult alternate plumage. Note the completely black hood and the all-black tail. The wing feathers are also all equally worn and all the same color.

Fig. 45. Audubon's Oriole, ASY bird

Figure 45. This is an ASY bird in adult alternate plumage. Note the complete black of the undertail. The adult male Scott's Oriole's undertail is yellow on the inner half and black on the outer edges.

Streak-backed Oriole

The Streak-backed Oriole is a medium-sized oriole with a thick straight bill and a relatively short rounded tail.

This is a Mexican oriole occasionally seen in south-eastern Arizona or southern California. It is unusual among our orioles in that the adult male and female have similar patterns of black on the face but differ in their body color.

Spot-breasted Oriole

This is a large oriole with a medium-length, thick, slightly downcurved bill.

In the United States, the Spot-breasted Oriole is found only in southeastern Florida, where it is seen in gardens and parks. The sexes look alike.

Fig. 46. Streak-backed Oriole, ASY female

Fig. 47. Spot-breasted Oriole, ASY bird

Figure 46. This is an ASY female in adult alternate plumage. The streaking on the back is just visible. The black mask, white-edged wing feathers, and dusky tail show this bird to be an adult. The yellowish head and body and dusky tail show that it is a female. The adult male would have a red-orange body and a black tail.

Figure 47. This is an ASY bird in adult alternate plumage. The black face and throat in combination with the spotting on the breast makes this Spot-breasted Oriole easily distinguishable from all of our other orioles. SY birds lack the black throat and may take a while to develop spots on the breast.

Oriole Population Trends

The First Step: Keeping Track

By keeping track of oriole populations over the years, we can get a sense of how well they are doing as a whole and how their ranges are expanding or contracting. Knowing that ranges or populations are changing and understanding why they are changing are two different things. The first is estimated through surveys; the second is largely conjecture, but important nonetheless. Clearly, before we try to interpret any change in population in a given year or two, it is important to look at the long term.

Below are brief comments on the population trends and changes in range of the eight oriole species that breed in the United States and, in some cases, into Canada. In addition, we have included maps for the five major species that show their relative abundance within their respective ranges. This data was gathered in summers over the last thirty years in what is called the Breeding Bird Survey (BBS). The different shades indicate the average number of orioles seen in each given area on the day of the annual survey.

Notes on Oriole Populations

Baltimore Oriole — Baltimore Oriole populations have shown fluctuations over the years but in the long run seem to be fairly stable. Baltimore Orioles breed in open areas with scattered trees or at the edges of forests, such as where a forest meets a field, stream, or road. Human development into forests creates edges and into plains adds suburban plantings. This creates more potential breeding habitat for this species. Thus, it is no surprise that over the last fifty years, Baltimore Orioles have

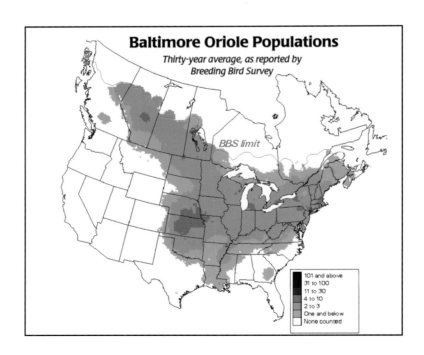

Baltimore Oriole Populations
Thirty-year average, as reported by Breeding Bird Survey

BBS limit

101 and above
31 to 100
11 to 30
4 to 10
2 to 3
One and below
None counted

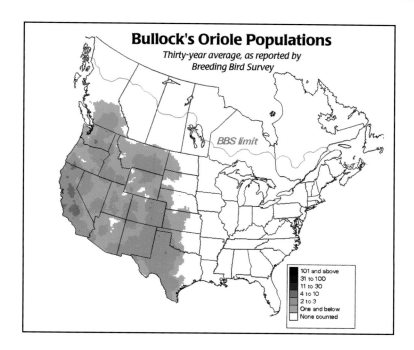

begun to expand their range into the Midwest and into northern areas such as the Upper Peninsula of Michigan.

At the same time, Baltimore Orioles seem to be receding from southern portions of their range where they used to breed regularly, such as Texas, Tennessee, and South Carolina.

Since the 1950s, Baltimore Orioles have expanded their winter range in the Southeast and Atlantic Coast. However, studies done in winter show declining numbers overall. It is possible that added backyard feeding has encouraged range expansion.

Orioles feed on caterpillars and other insects that they glean off trees, low shrubs, and occasionally the ground. In the past, when sprays such as DDT and Sevin were used to control insect pests, like the gypsy moth, this resulted in killing many Baltimore Orioles. Similarly, spraying lawns with any pesticide to kill insects must be regarded as a potential threat to orioles, since they may eat the sprayed insects.

Bullock's Oriole — The populations and breeding range of Bullock's Orioles seem to be fairly stable, but there are slight declines overall, especially in the West. Most Bullock's Orioles leave the United States during winter, but a few remain in southern California, and these numbers have been increasing slightly over the years.

Since Bullock's Orioles depend heavily on riparian habitat (the trees and vegetation along streams and rivers), preserving this corridor of vegetation in more arid areas is essential to their continued success. Any farming or ranching practices and conservation policies that preserve streamside and riverside vegetation will be beneficial to Bullock's Orioles. It will also benefit all other birds that live in the area and use riparian areas for breeding and/or migration stopovers.

Orchard Oriole — Populations of this species have been declining fairly steadily over the past thirty to forty years, especially in the western portion of their breeding range. For example, populations dropped by 40 percent in one decade in the south-central portion of its range. In Michigan, populations also dropped considerably — 1.5 percent each year from 1966 to 1989. These declines have placed it on the Special Concern list since 1982, a list of birds we must watch carefully to be sure they do not become threatened or endangered.

Like other orioles, the Orchard Oriole is susceptible to chemical spraying for insects. It is also a common host of both Brown-headed and Bronzed Cowbirds, especially in the South. These species may reduce its productivity, for they lay their eggs in the nest of the Orchard Oriole and often remove an

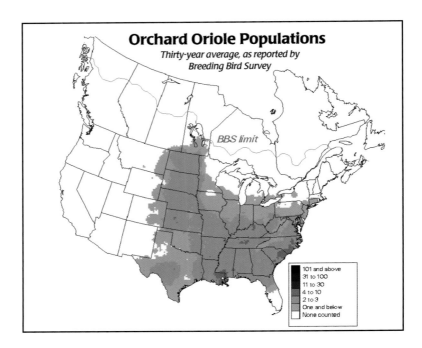

Orchard Oriole Populations
Thirty-year average, as reported by
Breeding Bird Survey

BBS limit

101 and above
31 to 100
11 to 30
4 to 10
2 to 3
One and below
None counted

oriole egg at the same time; the oriole then raises the cowbird's young along with its own.

Since the Orchard Oriole is a neotropical migrant (meaning that it winters in Central and South America and migrates north to breed), we also have to be concerned with its wintering grounds in the tropics, where it tends to be more restricted than the Baltimore Oriole in its altitudinal range, staying in lower altitudes. Any restriction like this leaves it more susceptible to habitat destruction.

Hooded Oriole — Populations of the Hooded Oriole have risen over the last forty years. The exception is southern Texas, where they seemed to have declined.

The Hooded Oriole has expanded its range into California, most likely in response to increasing urbanization and richer backyard plantings that provide food and nesting locations. In particular, the widespread urban use of the Washington fan palm in California may have had an effect, since this is by far the Hooded Oriole's favorite nesting tree in that region.

Scott's Oriole — Bird surveys show Scott's Oriole populations also rising over the last forty years. They have risen even more in western than eastern portions of their range.

Why this has occurred is not known. Possibly the

expansion of urban development into desert areas has provided more food and nesting opportunities.

Altamira Oriole — Altamira Orioles are mainly a Mexican species that just peeks over the border of southern Texas to breed, especially along the Rio Grande. At this time, there are about 125 nests in all of Texas.

The main threat to their population is habitat loss along the Rio Grande, especially where large trees have died or been removed. Altamira Orioles prefer to nest in the upper branches of tall trees that hang over open space. There are superb efforts to save this land along the river, and this may bode well for the Altamira Oriole.

Over the last decades, their populations seem to have shifted. They are declining in the eastern portion of their range, where they historically were numerous, and have increased in the western portion. Overall, there seems to be a decline in the last twenty years, but in the last five years their numbers may have leveled off.

Cold winters may reduce their numbers. Bronzed Cowbirds are also a factor. Second-year Altamiras may raise cowbird young in their nests, but adult Altamiras usually just abandon the nest when a cowbird has laid an egg in it.

Audubon's Oriole — This oriole seems to be

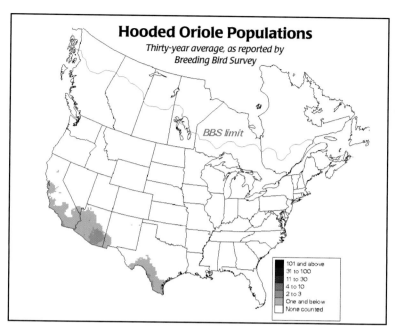

declining from the southern portion of its range along the Rio Grande valley, but it is not as habitat specific as the Altamira Oriole and also lives in the thorn scrub to the north.

Two reasons for its decline may be habitat fragmentation, where larger tracts of woods are broken into stands too small to support the breeding birds, and parasitism by the Bronzed Cowbird.

The Audubon's Oriole does not seem to be able to defend itself against cowbirds as well as Altamira Orioles. Perhaps it does not guard the nest as vigilantly; also, it does not nest near Great Kiskadees, as Altamiras do, which may keep cowbirds away.

Spot-breasted Oriole — Not much is known about the recent populations of Spot-breasted Orioles. Their range is small, and they nest in urban areas. Exceptionally cold weather in winter may kill some birds and reduce their populations, but then they seem to recover.

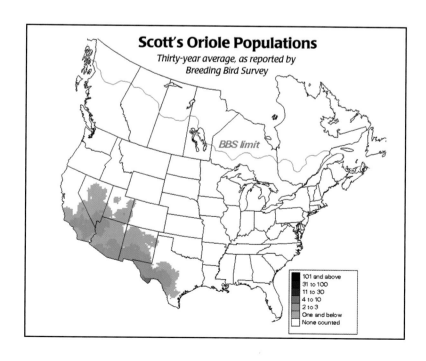

How You Can Help Orioles

What Difficulties Do Orioles Face?

The majority of our oriole species are what is termed neotropical migrants. This means that they migrate from temperate areas of the United States and Canada to tropical areas of Central and South America. Interestingly, orioles, like most other neotropical migrants, spend far less time with us on their breeding ground than they do on their wintering ground. Most orioles spend about 4 months with us during breeding, about 6–7 months in Central and South America wintering, and about 1–2 months in migration.

Neotropical migrants are dependent on three different habitats for their survival — the habitats where they breed, the habitats where they winter, and the habitats through which they migrate. They need food, shelter, and water in all of these, and additionally, they need nesting places and nesting materials where they breed.

Encroaching agricultural and urban development in all three habitats make the survival of neotropical migrants, like orioles, precarious and complicated.

Ways to Help Orioles

Preserve Habitats for Orioles — For orioles in the United States and Canada, critical issues of conservation are preserving patches of forested areas within urban development and re-creating and preserving forest edges along rivers and wetlands, often called riparian habitats. Riparian habitats are important for breeding orioles, since the orioles like the edges of the forests along rivers. They are also critical in arid areas of the West, where this may be the only vegetation with large trees and enough insects to sustain orioles during breeding and migration.

Buy Shade-Grown Coffee — In Central and South America, tall forest habitats are being destroyed at an alarming rate, mostly because of U. S. consumer demand for products. Forested areas are cleared to raise beef cattle, for instance. Also, because of increased demands for coffee around the world, coffee farmers have shifted from growing coffee in shaded conditions to cutting down surrounding trees and growing it in full sun. This destroys much of the winter habitat of orioles and many other songbirds that breed in the north, because they live and feed on the insects in the tall forest canopy.

There is a movement to encourage coffee farmers to let the trees stand and grow shade-grown coffee. You can look in your supermarket for companies that use shade-grown coffee; buying it helps the birds.

Avoid Using Pesticides — In all areas that orioles visit, whether wintering, breeding, or migrating, it is also extremely important that we not use pesticides in an attempt to kill certain insects. Orioles feed on these insects and can be harmed by the chemicals. A better idea is to attract orioles, for they are tremendous predators of many pest insects, like tent caterpillars and gypsy moths.

Celebrate International Migratory Bird Day — Because of the interest in neotropical migrants, the National Fish and Wildlife Foundation and the U.S. Fish and Wildlife Service helped start International Migratory Bird Day. It is celebrated each year on the second Saturday in May through festivals and events all across the country that try to raise people's awareness of neotropical migrant birds.

Orioles are really the poster bird for neotropical migrants, because they are colorful, popular, and so well known.

Emulate "the Other Orioles" — How could we write a book about orioles and not mention the Baltimore Orioles baseball team, which recently made their logo more realistic to better portray the bird? Along with the Fish and Wildlife Foundation and the Fish and Wildlife Service, the baseball Orioles have helped promote International Migratory Bird Day for the past several years at their ballpark. They hand out baseball cards with the birds on them and they show orioles on the scoreboard.

Keep Track of Orioles — People who feed orioles and provide nesting habitat get to see them all the time; they even get to see the young come to feeders later in the summer. But whether they come to feeders or not, you can keep track of orioles in your area by becoming more sensitive to their songs and calls. Most of our orioles have loud whistled songs that carry long distances, and in many of our species individuals have distinct song types that will enable you to recognize individuals in your neighborhood.

If you continue to listen for orioles throughout spring and summer, you will begin to know the centers of their activity and possibly even locate their nests. Often males and females give calls as they approach the nest.

Even in winter you can learn about the presence of orioles in your neighborhood by going out and looking for their nests hanging in the leafless trees. The nests are strong and last at least a year. This will help you know if a certain tree is a favorite nesting place in your yard or neighborhood park, and you can make sure it and others like it are saved. You can even start a small neighborhood watch for orioles with your neighbors. It is a good way to create a sense of community.

Keep a Journal — When and where you see orioles and how many you see can be important to people in the future. Records over time will not only be rewarding to you but also may be useful to others as we all try to follow the trends in oriole populations and the timings of their migration. Some

Male Baltimore Oriole perched on the spring flowers of a fruiting tree.

species are known to be declining by 1–2 percent a year. This may not sound like much, but over twenty years this is a decline of 20–40 percent.

Record how many orioles you see. Record when they come for food, what foods they eat, what you see them eat in the wild, whether they nest on your property, whether they raise young successfully, the first date of their arrival in spring, and the last date you see one in fall. All of this is interesting data that will help you learn more about orioles in your area.

Provide for Orioles' Needs — Most important, with the help of this book you can provide for the needs of orioles in your own backyard in a wide variety of ways. No matter what size your property, you can add feeders and create habitats that add wild foods; you can put out birdbaths; you can plant trees in which orioles like to build their nests; and you can provide the materials they need to build their nests.

All of these things will not only help the birds but also bring them into your yard, adding to your everyday enjoyment.

Sugar Water Feeders

It's Easy to Get Started

Attracting orioles is the fastest-growing new area of backyard bird feeding, and it is easy to be a participant. There are two key activities involved in attracting orioles. The first is to continually offer a wide variety of foods such as sugar water, fruit, and mealworms. The second is to make your property into as good an oriole habitat as possible by having nesting sites, nesting materials, wild fruits, and naturally occurring insects.

In this chapter, we tell you all about sugar water feeders. In the next chapter, we cover the other foods that you can feed orioles. Following chapters

Male Baltimore Oriole on the dried stalk of a mullein plant.

describe how to transform your property into a haven for orioles.

The Sugar Water Alternative

Orioles are attracted to feeders that offer sugar water solutions, because the concentrations of sugar mimic the nectar of flowers on which they naturally feed. Of course, though an alternative to flowers, sugar water feeders do not look like flowers, so it takes time for the orioles to learn that feeders are a new source of nectar. This was also true for hummingbirds, when hummingbird feeders were first used. In time, increasing numbers of birds learn how to use them.

Sugar water feeders attract a wide variety of other birds as well. Over fifty species of North American birds have been recorded visiting these feeders, including woodpeckers, finches, tanagers, and many others.

Most commercial feeders are designed to hold sugar water solutions, and a few have places to hold other foods too.

When and Where to Put Up Feeders

Migratory orioles arrive in the southern states in mid- to late March, and in the northern states and Canada they usually show up from late April to early May, depending on weather conditions.

Make sure you have your feeders up when the orioles first arrive, because the birds need to replenish their energy reserves after their long flight, and natural sources of food, like nectar, fruit, and insects, are often in short supply in spring. A study of Baltimore Orioles in Manitoba showed that females and males lost body mass during the first month

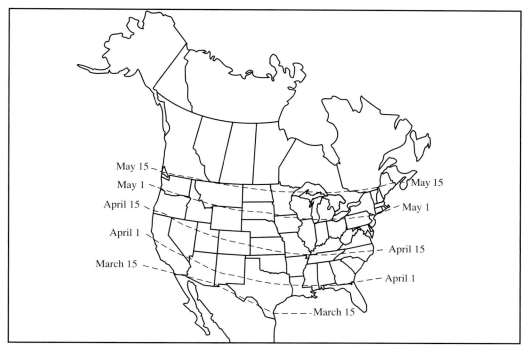

Spring Arrival Dates of Orioles

after arrival, suggesting that there was not enough food and that the birds were drawing on their fat reserves.

Leave the feeders up throughout the breeding season and take them down only after all orioles have migrated south, which is approximately mid-September. The stimulus for migration is changing day length, so having feeders up will not prevent orioles from migrating. If you live in an area where orioles can stay through the winter, such as southern California, the Southwest, southern Texas, and the Southeast, then be sure to leave them up.

Sugar water feeders can be hung or mounted on a pole, and they should always be placed near shrubs or trees, for this is where orioles naturally feed. You can place the feeders near your bird feeding station, in the garden, near a shrub border, or hanging from an apple or other fruit tree. Once the orioles have found your feeder, you can gradually place it closer to your house so you can have a better view of the birds.

If your orioles are already coming to one of your hummingbird feeders and you want to get them to go to an oriole feeder, remove the hummer feeder temporarily and put the oriole feeder in its place.

The birds get fixed on the location of the food source, and even if you removed all feeders they would come and hover over the spot. Once the orioles start using the oriole feeder, you can gradually move it to the desired spot and put the hummer feeder back.

Sugar Solutions

When offering sugar water solutions, naturally you want them to mimic the composition of flower nectar. Scientific studies of wildflowers have shown their nectar is largely composed of a type of sugar called sucrose and smaller amounts of glucose and dextrose in about a 21 percent concentration. White table sugar is essentially sucrose, so when mixed with water it makes a solution very like the nectar found in flowers.

The Recipe

Many people use a sugar water solution of 1 part white table sugar to 4 parts water (for example, 1 cup sugar to 4 cups water). However, many people successfully attract orioles with a solution of 1 part sugar to 5 or 6 parts water. We even know of people who attract orioles with a 1-to-8 sugar-to-water ratio. Experiment and see which your orioles prefer.

Never use brown sugar, honey, or artificial sweeteners in place of white table sugar. Honey ferments too easily and could harm the birds. Artificial sweeteners have no food value and do not give the birds the calories they need.

It is very important to boil the solution for 1 to 2 minutes and then to let it cool. Boiling helps retard fermentation and prevents spoiling, especially in hot weather. Store the unused portion of the solution in the refrigerator and make sure to change the solution every 2–3 days when the weather is warm. If the solution is spoiled, the orioles may not come to it.

As an alternative to homemade solutions, many manufacturers now offer commercial sugar mixtures that are premade; you just add the water. In some cases these mixtures have added nutrients; in other cases they are just sugar.

Commercial Feeders

Commercial feeders specifically designed for orioles are a recent invention. Before they were available, orioles came (and still come) to hummingbird feeders. But orioles are much larger than hummingbirds and often have to awkwardly contort themselves to cling to the feeder and reach the sugar; in the process they may tip the feeder and cause sugar water to spill out.

Oriole feeders have larger perches and landing areas to accommodate orioles' body sizes. The feeders are usually orange, according to the theory that orioles are attracted to the main color of their plumage and because they are known to come to cut orange halves. Manufacturers continue to improve upon the designs of these feeders, with new feeders coming out all the time.

One type of feeder is a large, 36-ounce-capacity egg-shaped feeder with bee-resistant feeding stations and specially designed perches that will fit any

Male Baltimore Oriole on a sugar water feeder made by Perky Pet Products.

Adult male Baltimore Oriole about to feed from a feeder made by Nature Products Inc.

size oriole, since oriole species vary somewhat in size.

Another feeder has a clever innovation that takes advantage of orioles' style of feeding and excludes bees. This 16-ounce saucer-shaped feeder has a cover with unique bee guards that look like the top of an orange half. These cover the feeding portals except for a tiny, thin vertical slit. Bees cannot get in, but orioles can insert their strong beaks, part the flexible material, and lap up the nectar. Additional tabs on the saucer help hold orange slices as an added enticement to the orioles.

You can also buy a combination feeder that has a covered saucer with feeding holes that give access to the sugar water. In addition, an orange half can be skewered on the hanger and there are little depressions on the saucer cover to hold fruit jelly.

Another new design is a 36-ounce feeder with perch-activated bee guards. Each perch is attached to an arm that covers the feeding hole with a round piece of plastic. There is a tiny hole in the plastic shield allowing hummingbirds to feed, but not bees. When an oriole lands, its weight pulls the perch down, revealing a larger feeding hole for the orioles.

Oriole feeders can be bought at wild bird specialty stores, lawn and garden stores, nature stores, hardware stores, and discount stores, and from specialty mail-order catalogs.

Homemade Feeders

Some people choose to make their own sugar water feeders for orioles out of household objects like wide-mouth jars that are not too deep. Other people have used hamster watering bottles from a pet store as feeders. Feeders can be painted orange or decorated with orange ribbon to attract the attention of the birds. Attach feeders to trees, posts, or other places where orioles can land.

Cleaning Feeders

It is important to keep feeders impeccably clean and refilled every few days, especially in warm weather. This is because sugar water solutions can spoil and mold, and this may harm the birds.

Most feeders are easy to clean. Take off the top and rinse out the inside in hot water. You can use

Male Hooded Oriole at a feeder.

some vinegar mixed in the hot water to remove mold; for tough jobs use a tiny amount of chlorine bleach in the hot water. Wipe around with a sponge. You may need to use a tiny brush to clean out the portals; these are available from the makers of hummingbird feeders. Do not use harsh or abrasive cleaners, for they could scratch the plastic parts. Make sure you rinse out the feeder thoroughly before refilling.

When Will Orioles Use Feeders?

In warmer areas of the country, like southern California, southern Texas, and the Gulf Coast, where orioles can be found throughout the year, they come to feeders in all months. One woman in Tallahassee, Florida, has been feeding orioles from January through March for three years. She has had up to five Baltimore Orioles at once visit her feeders, which offer such varied foods as sugar water, jelly, and a homemade suet mixture.

In areas where orioles are migratory, people report differing results with feeders. Some see orioles coming to feeders throughout the breeding season, from spring through late summer, and even bringing their young to the feeders. Others report orioles coming to their feeders mainly in spring.

Why do some orioles visit feeders only in the spring? It may be because when they first arrive insects are scarce and the orioles are hungry. Once they establish breeding territories and start raising young, they may need to shift from eating sugar water to eating protein. Insects have a higher protein content than sugar water and fruit, which have virtually none, and protein is necessary for nestling growth and feather development. Scientific studies of Bullock's Orioles show that up to 79 percent of their food during the breeding season is adult and larval insects, especially caterpillars.

Another possible explanation for orioles coming to feeders only in spring is that they may be migrants who are just passing through, who will establish breeding areas elsewhere. In some areas of the West, for instance, orioles mostly nest in riparian habitats, such as in willows along streams. If you are far from these areas, orioles may visit your feeders only in passing.

Even when there is suitable nesting habitat, ori-

Male Bullock's (right) and female Hooded Oriole at an Opus feeder.

oles may still come and then move. We once had a Baltimore Oriole briefly come to eat cut oranges in our backyard. A few days later it moved to our neighbor's property, where it built a nest and raised a family. It did not return to our yard except in later summer, when we saw it feeding fledglings from our raspberry bushes.

Another way to entice orioles to feeders throughout the breeding season is to offer other kinds of food, like mealworms, which are a good protein source. See the next chapter for more on this.

Other Tips

Here are some other tips for attracting orioles to your feeders and understanding their behavior.

Orioles Need to Learn About Feeders — Remember that orioles first have to find your feeder and recognize it as a food source. Some orioles have obviously learned this and others have not. It may be that as more people feed orioles and more birds learn to use and bring their young to the feeders, the number of feeder-wise orioles will increase exponentially. This is what has happened with hummingbirds.

Get Their Attention Early — Make sure you have the feeders up just as or right before the orioles arrive from migration, because they may be actively searching for food then, and they may be apt to explore new food sources. Also, keep the feeders filled with fresh unspoiled solution and make sure the fruit is fresh.

You May Not See Them — Remember that you may have orioles on your property and just not see them. When orioles first arrive in many areas in spring, the leaves are not out and the birds are more visible. Later, after leaf-out, the birds may be harder to see and spending more time in the tops of the tree canopy nesting. Also, orioles may still be coming to the feeders, but not as frequently.

Prevent Pilfering by Bees and Ants — Bees and ants are also attracted to sugar water solutions. Several oriole feeders come with built-in protection from bees and wasps. Another tactic is to rub a little salad oil around (not in) the feeding hole so that bees cannot get a foothold. Many oriole feeders also come with a built-in ant cup, a little moat filled with water that surrounds the wire from which the feeder hangs. The concept is that ants cannot swim across the water to get to the feeder. If your feeder does not have this feature, separate ant cups are now sold commercially.

Oranges, Mealworms, and More

It's Not All Sugar Water

There are many other ways to entice orioles to your yard besides sugar water feeders. Orioles are attracted to a wide range of other foods, and since the hobby of feeding orioles is still in its infancy, there is still lots of experimenting to do. Here are a few proven ways that include fruits, jellies, suet, and mealworms.

Male Baltimore Oriole at orange feeder.

Oranges

Orioles seem to be irresistibly drawn to oranges. They perch nearby or sometimes cling to the edge of the orange and devour the juicy flesh. The easiest way to offer oranges is to slice one in half and put the halves outside on a deck railing, platform bird feeder, or other area where they will be easily seen by the orioles. You can also hammer a nail into a tree and impale the orange half on it (make a little hole in the bottom of the orange first so that it goes on easily).

There are also convenient, commercially manufactured hanging wooden holders for orange halves. They consist of a vertical wooden board with a dowel sticking through it on which orange halves can be fixed. There are also perches on which the birds can land. Some even have a little metal cup to hold jelly.

The same advice about offering sugar water applies here. Offer oranges where the birds can see them and you can see the birds, and try putting them in several locations to increase the likelihood that orioles will find them. Plan to have the oranges out right before or right as the orioles arrive. Check the migration map on page 35 for the time orioles arrive in your area.

How long orioles will come to oranges depends on where you live, the species of orioles in your area, and habits of individual birds. In some cases, orioles stop coming to oranges and shift their attention to sources of protein, like insects. In other cases, orioles continue to come to oranges throughout the breeding season, or all year if you live in areas where orioles are found year-round.

Male Baltimore Oriole feeding on orange half.

Other Fruit

In addition to oranges, orioles also come to watermelon, grapefruit, apple slices, raisins, cherries, bananas, peaches, and even cactus fruits. Experiment and see which fruits orioles in your area like best. Do not be surprised if other birds are attracted to the fruit. Birds such as Western, Summer, and Scarlet Tanagers, Verdins, flickers, Gila and Red-bellied Woodpeckers, sapsuckers, grosbeaks, thrashers, Northern Mockingbirds, Northern Cardinals, Pyrrhuloxias, and Carolina Wrens have been attracted by fruit.

Grape Jelly

It's no surprise that orioles, being fruit lovers, are attracted to fruit jelly. In some places, orioles continue coming to jelly all summer, after they have stopped coming to oranges. We have found that they are especially fond of grape jelly, but they come to other flavors as well. One woman we know has had excellent results offering orange marmalade to the orioles in her yard.

The trick is to find a good way to offer the jelly. We buy small plastic containers in the grocery store that are about 2 inches high and 2 1/4 inches in diameter. We fill them with jelly and place them on a small hanging tray at our bird feeding station. We also put orange halves next to them. In addition to orioles, we have a pair of Gray Catbirds that have developed a real fondness for the jelly and have been coming to it for the last three years.

Some people fill empty orange halves with grape jelly after the orioles have cleaned out the pulp. We have heard of other people who melt the jelly until it turns to liquid, then dilute it one to one with water. This needs to be offered in a small cup.

Remember to keep the jelly fresh by changing it and cleaning its container every several days so that it will not spoil.

Mealworms — The Next Frontier

A relatively new and unexplored food source for attracting orioles is mealworms. We think this has the potential to become a very popular way to attract orioles and, for that matter, a wide variety of other birds as well.

The advantages of mealworms are that they are a source of protein and closely resemble caterpillars, which are a favorite and important wild food of orioles throughout the breeding season. Orioles need to feed their young protein for effective and proper development.

Mealworms are the larval stage of the yellow mealworm *(Tenebrio molitor)*, a type of grain beetle.

They look like short, thin, smooth, brown caterpillars that are 3/4 inch long. They are sold in pet stores and wild bird specialty stores. Mealworms are also sold by mail order (see Resources, page 94).

Mealworms are bought or shipped in plastic containers and can be stored in the refrigerator, where they remain dormant and can last 3–12 months. Take out as many as you need at a time; you can use tweezers to pick them up if you wish. A single bird could easily eat 50 in a single day. Most people order quantities of 100 to 500. We know of one enthusiast who buys 5,000 at a time and even bought a small college-dorm-type refrigerator just to store her mealworms. She feeds them to her bluebirds.

Female Baltimore Oriole eating grape jelly.

Male Baltimore Oriole entering feeder offering mealworms.

How to Offer

Try to put the mealworms out consistently at the same time of day so the birds will become accustomed to finding this food source. Mealworms can be offered in a cup or dish (with somewhat high sides so they can't climb out). Put the container on a feeding tray, platform, or other area where orioles can find it.

We know someone in Wisconsin who has an ingenious device for offering mealworms to orioles. It is a wooden platform feeder with a boxlike covering of wire mesh. The wire mesh is vinyl-coated, and the openings in it are 2 x 2 inches. Inside the boxed area is a dish that holds the mealworms. The 2 x 2 openings allow orioles to get through but keep out larger birds that might steal all the mealworms.

The man who devised the feeder got the orioles to find the mealworms initially by putting orange halves on top of the wire. The orioles would land, look through the wire, and see the mealworms. Eventually, they went in to get them. Both Baltimore and Orchard Orioles come throughout the breeding season, and they even bring their young to the feeder.

This wire cage is a good device, since one of the "problems" with mealworms is that they are so attractive to so many birds. The cage can keep larger birds like jays, grackles, and crows from eating the mealworms, and saves a few for smaller birds like orioles, warblers, and so forth.

Suet

Suet is a special fat found near the kidneys of cattle. Some people have great success feeding orioles suet mixes. There are now commercially available orange-flavored suet blocks that orioles particularly seem to enjoy and come to feed at throughout the breeding season. You can offer the commercial blocks of suet in the handy wire containers that can be hung out at a feeding station. The orioles can grab onto the wire mesh as they feed. There are other fruit-flavored suet blocks as well; experiment with your orioles to see what they like best. Some people make their own suet mixtures, but we find that the commercially sold blocks are convenient and hold up better in warm weather.

Providing Wild Foods for Orioles

What and How Orioles Eat

The wild food of orioles consists of three main things: insects, fruit, and nectar. In general, these three foods groups are used in varying proportions through the year in accordance with their relative abundance. In most cases, insects make up the majority of food in spring and early summer during breeding; fruits compose more of their diet from midsummer into fall, when fruits have ripened; and nectar is taken whenever nectar flowers are in bloom, which is mostly in spring and summer. On their wintering grounds in the tropics, they feed largely on insects and nectar.

Orioles are in the family Icteridae, sometimes called blackbirds. This includes grackles, blackbirds, meadowlarks, orioles, and cowbirds in the United States and Canada. This whole family is evolved to do a special type of feeding called gaping, in which a bird places its closed bill into a food source and then opens it, or "gapes," to expose or break into the food. Of course, all birds can open their bills, but these birds have evolved especially strong muscles for opening their bills, rather than just for closing them.

Male Hooded Oriole on an agave plant from which it may drink the nectar.

Male Baltimore Oriole in spring flowers.

Other groups of birds adapted to this mode of feeding include crows, jays, and starlings.

If you see grackles or starlings feeding on a lawn, go and look at where they fed. You will find little holes where the grass has been pushed back. These are places where they poked in their closed bill, gaped, then looked for insects.

It is believed that the short bristly feathers in the area between the eye and bill (the lores) of the blackbird family are dark to keep reflected light from interfering with their seeing prey items where they have gaped. You will also note that many of our orioles have black on the face in this region or black or charcoal specifically on the lores.

Orioles use gaping in several ways. They use it to pry into curled leaves when looking for caterpillars. They may use it to eat hairy or spiny caterpillars like tent caterpillars; rather than eating the whole larva, spines and all, they gape into its body and lick the juices with their tongue. Gaping is also used to eat fruits and the nectar of flowers. In the case of flowers, they poke into the base of the flower, gape to push aside the petals and sepals, and then lick up the nectar.

Growing Fruits

Orioles feed on a variety of fruits, and by planting these in your yard you will increase your chances of attracting orioles. A way to do this and save the cost of a new plant is first to take a brief walk around your yard to see what fruiting plants you may already have. Often there is one being shaded or crowded out by other plants and thus not very productive. Simply replant it to a better spot and give it a feeding of compost, and it will produce for you and the orioles.

Small fruits that orioles eat include cherry, mul-

Male Hooded Oriole at red-hot poker flowers, where it will feed on nectar.

berry, raspberry, blackberry, juneberry, hawthorne, and elderberry. In many cases, such as cherries, orioles will not swallow the whole fruit as a robin would, but just perch on the branch and eat small pieces at a time, leaving the fruit attached to the tree.

Orioles eat larger fruits as well, by gaping. Large fruits that orioles regularly eat include apple, pear, peach, apricot, grape, and orange. Orioles in desert regions have also been observed eating cactus fruits.

Attract Orioles and Reduce Pest Insects

The three main groups of insects that orioles eat are moth caterpillars, grasshoppers, and beetles. In addition to these, they eat ants, bees, and bugs. Other animal foods include spiders, snails, and an occasional lizard.

In most cases, you do not have to attract these insects. For example, most of us do not have to attract tent caterpillars and other destructive moth larvae, we already have them. The good news is that if you have them, orioles will be attracted and reduce their numbers year after year.

Orioles are particularly effective in reducing infestations of tent caterpillars, fall webworms, and gypsy moths, in the last case eating both the caterpillars and pupae. They also eat tussock moths, browntail moths, and cankerworms. The caterpillars from all of these moths are major defoliators of fruit and shade trees.

Orioles also eat many beetles, especially weevils, that feed on commercial crops like cotton and trees like walnuts and pecans, which can be both commercial and decorative.

Though orioles will reduce grasshoppers' numbers as well, these insects are not a problem for most homeowners. In midsummer, listen for their trills and buzzing sounds and try to preserve some of the habitat they seem to like on your property. This is often some area with longer grasses, an area rich with wild plants and weeds, or a tangle of shrubs and vines. By leaving these areas alone, you can make your property more attractive to crickets and grasshoppers and a better place for orioles to feed.

Though we said this earlier, it bears repeating: because orioles eat so many insects and feed them to their young, it is extremely important not to use any pesticides on your property in an attempt to eliminate insects. Do not spray your trees or shrubs for caterpillars or your lawn for beetles. It has been shown that spraying these insects can cause direct harm or even death to orioles and other birds, like bluebirds, that attempt to feed on sprayed insects. Let the orioles take care of the pests for you.

Flowers for Nectar

The first orioles we see in our own backyard every spring are Baltimore and Orchard Orioles as they sit among the newly opened apple blossoms, drinking nectar from the flowers. All orioles will drink nectar from flowers. If the flowers are small, like apple blossoms, the birds will just reach in from the top. If the flowers are larger, like trumpet creeper, they may poke into the base of the flower, gape to open a space between the sepals and petals, and then lap up the nectar.

Flowers that orioles have been known to visit for nectar include apple, cherry, peach, trumpet creeper, lily, eucalyptus, ocotillo, queen's bird of paradise, agave, aloe, and hibiscus. During spring migration in Florida, Orchard Orioles have been seen to feed in great numbers at the blossoms of black locust; however, it is not known whether they were getting nectar or actually eating some of the blossoms. In California, when orioles feed on eucalyptus blossoms, it is believed that they eat both nectar and pollen.

There may be many other flowers that orioles love. Observe and experiment on your own property. Keep in mind that the flowers mentioned above all have fairly large stems that can support the weight of the oriole as it feeds. Flowers with weak stems may not work, since the orioles cannot perch on them and are unable to hover and feed like a hummingbird.

Habitats and Trees for Nesting Orioles

Oriole Nests

Orioles build hanging or semihanging nests, and these require trees with the right branching structure to make them work. Most orioles build nests in a wide variety of trees, but as we studied the eight species that breed in North America, we began to see that certain trees and situations are favored by each

species. And sometimes these preferences change in different regions of a single species' range.

In this chapter we describe, species by species, what kinds of habitats they prefer and the trees they favor, so that in managing your property you will have the greatest chance of attracting orioles.

Habitat and Nest Tree Preferences

Baltimore Oriole — Baltimore Orioles nest in open woodlands, orchards, rural and suburban areas with shade trees, and forest edges, such as along streams, rivers, and roads.

In the first half of the 1900s, the favorite nesting tree of Baltimore Orioles was the American elm. They loved finding an isolated elm in a suburban or rural yard and the safety of building their hanging nest at the tips of the arching branches. At that time, when driving down a tree-lined street in winter, it was common to see oriole nests hanging above the road from the leafless trees.

Since about 1950, however, the elms have been attacked by Dutch elm disease and are no longer common. Baltimore Orioles have had to shift to other trees.

In the North, their favorite trees are now the maples — silver, sugar, and red — oaks, poplars, willows (including weeping willow), and apple. In the northernmost part of their range they also use birch. In the South, they seem to prefer sycamores, pecans, and live oaks. In the Midwest, they use mostly maple, poplar, willow, birch, and oak.

Baltimore Orioles, like most other orioles, prefer deciduous trees to conifers, but occasionally they will nest in trees such as spruce and hemlock.

Bullock's Oriole — The habitat of Bullock's Orioles is similar to that of Baltimore Orioles. They

This palm tree is good Hooded Oriole nesting habitat.

Male Baltimore Oriole guarding his nest while the female is away.

nest in open woodlands, along forest edges, in streamside trees, and around rural and suburban settlements. Bullock's Orioles also nest in a wide variety of trees, but in each region of their range certain trees are repeatedly used more than others.

In the Southwest, the most popular trees are mesquite, sycamore, cottonwood, willow, and pecan. Where mistletoe grows on the trees in this region, Bullock's Orioles may build their nest right inside the bunches of this parasitic plant. North into the Great Plains, Bullock's Orioles use mostly cotton-

woods. This makes sense since these are one of the dominant trees along rivers and streams in the Midwest.

In California, Bullock's Orioles nesting in orchards use peach, pear, almond, and apple; along rivers they use willows, sycamores, and cottonwoods; and in upland areas they use oak, eucalyptus, and mulberry.

In the northernmost portion of their range they nest in birch, quaking aspen, cottonwood, and some conifers.

Perfect nesting habitat for many species of orioles — tall trees at water's edge.

Orchard Oriole — Areas with a mixture of open space and dense shrubs or taller trees are preferred by Orchard Orioles. These habitats include second-growth forests, brushy hillsides, orchards, and scattered trees in rural or suburban settings.

True to their name, Orchard Orioles often nest in areas of fruit trees such as apple, peach, and pear. These trees are shorter than other shade trees, and this is fine with Orchard Orioles. They tend to nest lower than Baltimore Orioles, with which their range overlaps.

Besides orchard trees, Orchard Orioles in the North prefer to nest in willow, cottonwood, and maple. They also may nest in a shrub called button-bush, which grows only about 6–8 feet tall. In the South, they prefer to nest in live oak, pecan, sycamore, magnolia, and longleaf pine.

Along the Gulf Coast, a substantial number of Orchard Orioles may nest in *Phragmites communis*, the tall grasses of marshy areas. This grass grows 8–10 feet tall, and the nests are secured to several stems and hang down between them.

In Texas, Orchard Orioles nest in mesquite, willow, hackberry, cedar elm, retama, live oak, honey locust, and pecan.

Hooded Orioles — Hooded Orioles can nest in a variety of habitats. In dry scrub, they usually choose mesquite for their nest building. Along rivers, they prefer sycamore and cottonwood.

Early accounts of Hooded Oriole breeding behavior described their nests as frequently being inside growths of mistletoe, with a lining of dark hairlike moss. In recent decades, they seem to have changed to nesting most frequently in palmetto and palm, where they sew their nest to the underside of the large green leaves for protection.

This is often the case when they nest around

human settlements, whether it be ranches, suburbs, or city parks. This is particularly true in California, where their most common nesting tree is the fan palm, *Washingtonia filifera,* a palm widely planted in cities, parks, and suburban yards. Banana trees planted in landscapes are used for nesting by Hooded Orioles in the same way. Other nesting trees used near human settlements include eucalyptus, walnut, cypress, and cottonwood.

Scott's Oriole — Several habitats suit Scott's Orioles in the semiarid environment of their range. These include low mountain areas of piñon pines and juniper, canyons with oak and sycamore, grasslands with yuccas, and Joshua tree habitat.

In areas where there are a great many yuccas, they will nest almost exclusively in these plants. One study of 214 nests in western Texas found all but one nest to be in Thompson's yucca, *Yucca rostrata.* In other areas, they prefer to nest in Joshua tree, sycamore, live oak, and pine.

Altamira Oriole — These orioles live in open forests and forest edges primarily along the Rio Grande valley. They prefer to nest in tall trees and at the tips of branches that hang out into the open. Thus, nests are often built at forest edges or where trees arch over a river, road, or other open space. In these areas they nest especially in ash, cedar elm, hackberry, Texas persimmon, leadtree, and acacia.

Audubon's Oriole — Audubon's Orioles live in deciduous forests along the Rio Grande and slightly farther north into thorn scrub. In the river areas they nest in a wide variety of trees, and in the brushland they prefer mesquite.

Spot-breasted Oriole — This species lives in heavily planted urban and suburban areas along the southeast coast of Florida. They nest in a variety of tall native and exotic trees in these areas.

Female Bullock's Oriole feeding young at nest.

Providing Nesting Materials

Basic Needs of Birds

Attracting birds requires that you understand the needs of the species you are trying to attract. For orioles, providing the right breeding habitat and nesting trees is the first step in getting them to breed in your yard. But another equally important thing you can do is provide the right nesting materials. The availability and even just the sight of these materials can often stimulate a bird to start nest building and to breed in your area.

Oriole Nests

All of our orioles build nests that are basically a hanging basket suspended from the tips of branches or suspended between several branches. Their nests have two basic types of materials: long strands of material used in the outer construction and shorter strands and downy materials used in the lining. The specific materials used vary slightly from species to species.

In this chapter we will go over the favored nesting materials for each species, suggest how you can provide these naturally through growing plants, and then show how you can also offer substitute nesting materials.

Nests and Nest Materials of North American Orioles

Baltimore Oriole — Baltimore Orioles make a hanging nest that is about 4–8 inches long and usually placed 25–30 feet above the ground. The most common materials used for the construction of the nest are the outer bark from milkweed (*Asclepias* spp.) and Indian hemp or dogbane (*Apocynum* spp.). These wild plants are perennials whose stalks remain standing through winter. The next spring, when Baltimore Orioles are ready to build, the bark has weathered and can be pulled off by the birds in long strands that are extremely strong. These strands are silvery gray and form the dominant color of Baltimore Oriole nests. Two other materials they use in lesser quantities are grape bark, which also comes

Female Baltimore Oriole getting nesting material from a suet holder.

Female Baltimore Oriole at basket containing a variety of nest materials.

off the plant in thin strips, and Spanish moss in the South.

Baltimore Orioles have proved resourceful in their use of nest materials and will accept many substitutes for these natural plant fibers, including horsehair, human hair, string, yarn, cloth strips, and even odd bits of trash.

For the inner lining of the nest they use shorter fibers and downy material. These include the seed dispersal filaments of dandelions, willows, and poplars, occasional feathers, and short strips of grape bark.

You can grow milkweed and dogbane in an open sunny area of your yard. Just be sure to leave the old stalks standing through winter and into the next summer, for it is from these old stalks that orioles get the bark. You can also encourage any grapevines on your property. Willows, poplars, and aspens not only will provide lining material, they are also trees that Baltimore Orioles like to build in. Even dandelions become a good thing, for they provide nest lining material!

Bullock's Oriole — Bullock's Orioles construct a

Female Baltimore Oriole at the early stages of nest building.

hanging nest that is about 4–6 inches long and suspended from branch tips 15–25 feet above the ground.

The nests are built of plant fibers, especially from plants in the flax genus (*Linum* spp.), and sometimes fibers from palms (especially in California). They also use horsehair, twine, and grass. The lining materials include feathers, downy dispersal fibers from cottonwoods and willows, horsehair, and wool.

Having cottonwoods and willows for Bullock's Orioles not only provides nest lining materials but also nesting trees, for these are some of their favorite nest trees throughout much of their range. You can grow flax in your garden, and palms can be a nice addition to a landscape in the right climate.

Orchard Oriole — These orioles build a nest that is 3–4 inches long and placed 10–20 feet above the ground. Rather than being suspended from branch tips like many other oriole nests, it is hung from a fork in a horizontal limb.

Unlike Baltimore Orioles, Orchard Orioles build their nests almost exclusively of long thin grasses. The grasses are green when the nest is built and then dry to a characteristic golden yellow. Two types of grass that have been identified in these nests are mesquite grass (*Bouteloua* spp.) and salt-meadow grass *(Spartina patens),* although undoubtedly others are used. In the South, Orchard Orioles sometimes build their nests inside bunches of hanging Spanish moss.

Nest lining materials include cattail fluff and willow seed dispersal filaments.

Since fresh long grasses are essential to the Orchard Oriole's nest construction, it would be important for you to let a variety of grasses grow tall on your property in spring and early summer and not to cut them down.

Hooded Oriole — Hooded Orioles build a hanging nest 4 inches long and often sewn to the underside of fresh palm leaves anywhere from 5 to 45 feet above the ground. They sometimes build within bunches of mistletoe, but more commonly attach the nest to palm or banana leaves. They use wiry grasses, yucca fibers, and fibers from palms and palmettos to build the nest. In California, they show more of a tendency to use just palm fibers.

Obviously, growing palms and yuccas in your yard could be the first step in attracting this species within its range.

Scott's Oriole — This species builds a shallow nest that is 2–4 inches long and suspended at the rim from branches or sewn to the leaves of yucca. Many nests are constructed almost entirely from fibers pulled from yucca leaves.

However, not all yuccas produce fibers that can be pulled off and utilized by the birds. In one study in western Texas, the two species utilized by Scott's Orioles were Spanish dagger *(Yucca treculeana)* and giant dagger *(Y. faxoniana).* Scott's Orioles will also use mesquite grasses and other grasses in the construction of their nests. Horsehair is used in the exterior and in the lining, along with downy plant fibers.

Altamira Oriole — The most spectacular nest of all our orioles is the Altamira's. It is suspended from branches or occasionally power lines and is up to 25 inches long. The nest usually hangs 12–50 feet above the ground.

The birds use a variety of construction materials, including palmetto fibers, the inner bark of a variety of trees and vines, Spanish moss, wild flax, horse-

hair, and the rootlets of epiphytes. The lining is made of horsehair, plant down, grasses, wool, and feathers.

Audubon's Oriole — Audubon's Orioles build a hanging nest that is about 3 inches long and often placed in a mesquite tree 6–15 feet above the ground. Nest materials are similar to those of the Orchard Oriole — mostly green grasses that then dry to a yellow color. It may be lined with finer grasses and downy plant material.

Spot-breasted Oriole — This species builds a hanging nest about 4–8 inches long attached to the tips of branches 15–40 feet above the ground, depending a great deal on the type of vegetation available in its mainly urban habitat. Not much is known about its nesting materials.

Providing Your Own Nesting Materials

Besides growing the plants that orioles use in constructing their nests, you can also collect nesting materials elsewhere and offer them to the birds in spring.

The best way to offer nesting materials is in a suet basket that has an open wire mesh. Place the materials — horsehair, milkweed bark, etc. — inside and hang the basket in a prominent spot where the orioles may see it. Place it near your oriole feeders, or in a tree that is a favorite nest tree species, or just on a pole placed out in the middle of your yard. You will probably find that other species of birds besides orioles take an interest in it as well.

You can also offer human materials, such as lengths of string or yarn about 1 foot long. These could even be draped across the railing of a deck to attract the birds. If placing out artificial materials, be sure to avoid offering any monofilament fishing line. The birds can become tangled in it and have trouble getting free.

Also, if you like to fish, do not leave fishing line lying around. Many orioles live along rivers, and they will be attracted to the line as a nesting material. Besides the possibility of entangling themselves, orioles may spend inordinate amounts of time and energy trying to nip pieces and not be able to.

How an Oriole Builds Its Nest

What Is a Nest?

Many people think of a nest as a home. But for birds it is really just a container and a nursery. From the time it is built to the end of egg laying, the adults do not stay in it, during either the day or the night. Once the eggs are laid, its function is to hold the eggs and contain the young as they develop. The first time a parent stays in the nest is when incubation starts, and that is done only by the female.

Once the young are able to leave the nest, they do so, and no members of the family return to use the nest again.

The Roles of the Sexes

Among orioles, it is the female that does all of the nest building. Occasionally the male may bring a strand or two to the nest site, but he rarely participates in the actual building. There are reports of male Baltimore Orioles building nests, but this is most likely a result of the observer's mistaking an older female, possibly with a black head, for a male. There have been occasions when males have helped weave material, but these are definitely exceptions.

The main role of the male during nest building is to watch over the female while she makes all of the

Altamira Oriole adding to its pendant nest.

trips collecting material. He stays 10–20 feet away and makes sure that no other males mate with her, for nest building is the time when he will mate with her.

The Building Process

One of the few published accounts of oriole nest building was written by Francis Hobart Herrick in 1935. We have summarized his observations in this account.

At first the female brings long strands of material, one at a time, and loosely wraps them over the chosen branches. They may be wrapped with 1–2 turns or just laid over the branch. As more strands are added, some of the strands become more tightly connected to each other and to the support. This soon results in a hanging mass of strands.

In following trips, the bird brings other strands and pokes them through the hanging mass, "shuttling" them with sideways movements of her bill. She may even hang upside down from the supporting branch while doing this. At the same time, she may poke or pull other loose ends already there.

As the building progresses, the female makes more shuttling movements during each trip, sometimes up to a hundred thrusts and pulls, all very rapid. No deliberate knots are made, and the strand that is poked in is not necessarily the one that is pulled through in the next movement. Thus, there does not seem to be any deliberate weaving.

All of this results in a connected mass of strands and dangling ends that will be one wall of the nest. She then starts to lay strands over an adjacent branch in the same manner as before, to create another wall like the first. Then she shuttles additional strands through both sides and brings up loose ends and shuttles them through as well. This joins the two sides into a rough basket.

She then begins to enter this mass through the top and press her breast against the sides to help mold and shape the interior of the nest. More poking and drawing are done from the inside, probably strengthening the structure. Finally, she brings in finer materials that make up the nest lining. The whole process takes 5–8 days.

The ability to build the nest is all instinctive and never learned. Orioles build a new nest for each brood, never reusing a nest from a previous brood or

Baltimore Oriole checking the eggs in its nest.

previous years. However, they will take nesting materials from old nests and even steal them from other species' nests.

Winter Nests

Oriole nests are incredibly strong and long lasting. In fact, where orioles build in deciduous trees, it can be fun to look for their nests in winter when the leaves have fallen. This is an interesting way to do a little census of the nesting orioles in your area. These nests can last through all of the winter storms and into the next summer.

A Day in the Life of an Oriole

The Value of Observations

It is amazing how rarely any human takes time to observe an animal for more than a few minutes. This is particularly true in the case of our native birds, about which there is still so much to learn.

What follows is just a small example of notes we took while watching the nest of a Baltimore Oriole in an ash tree in our neighbor's front yard. We started around 10 AM and finished around 4:30 PM and were sitting out in the open about 60 feet from the nest. Interspersed with our notes are some comments we added later to highlight certain behaviors.

Male Baltimore Oriole feeding young at nest.

You can try this exercise yourself. It is just one day's effort, but it will provide you with a lifetime memory, a rare insight into the life of a bird, and most likely glimpses of behaviors that have rarely been seen before.

Bird Diary

10:00 — Male arrives with food and sings once. Enters nest and feeds young. Can hear young calling from 40 yards away. Male leaves with fecal sac in his bill. *(A fecal sac is droppings in a thin membrane; nature's diaper service).*

10:09 — Male arrives with food; young call. Male feeds young and sings once as he leaves.

10:10 — Eastern Kingbird lands in nest tree; flies off.

10:17 — Female arrives with food; silent. Feeds young and leaves.

10:18 — Male arrives with food; sings twice; feeds young. Gives "wheet wheet wheet" call and "churrr" call. Leaves.

10:19 — Female sings a 4-note song; 3 repeated notes and then 1 lower note. Also heard a 6-note song; 3 repeated notes, a lower note, a higher note, and a lower note; not sure who sang it.

Comment: Male and female seem to be sharing equally in the feeding here. Also, they are quite noisy around the nest, singing and calling almost every time they arrive.

10:22 — Male arrives with food; sings twice; after feeding young, comes out of nest and wipes bill. Leaves.

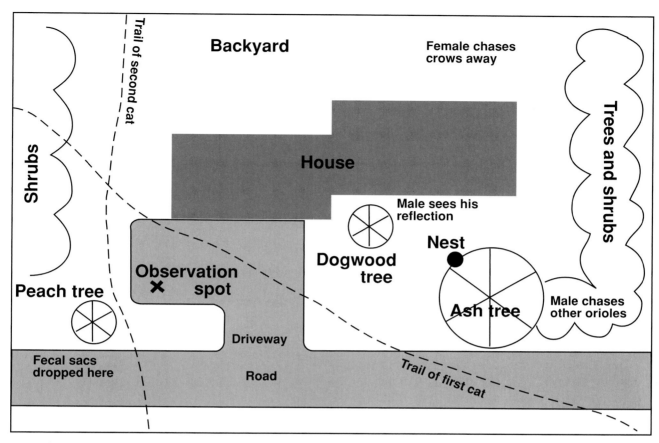

Map of Where Orioles Lived

10:30 — Female arrives; feeds young; sings; quivers wings. Male arrives; female chatters, sings, quivers wings, spreads tail and lifts it to a 45-degree angle. Both leave nest area.

10:37 — Male arrives with food; sings; feeds young; sings. Flies to ground chasing another male Baltimore Oriole that was there; chases the other oriole 50–100 yards.

10:40 — Female arrives with food; sings song exactly like male. Young start calling when adult lands on branch that holds nest; possibly song and then jiggling of branch stimulates them to call. We notice that the pattern of dark on female's head comes down into a V on her throat.

10:42 — Female arrives with food; feeds young; sings after feeding young — 4-note song.

10:46 — Male arrives with food; sings after feeding young; song is 1–3 notes longer than female's song.

Comment: At this point we have recognized the differences in the songs of this male and female. Each individual's songs are fairly consistent, so if a new oriole sang in the area, we would know it was a newcomer.

11:09 — Young calling from nest while parents are away.

11:12 — Female arrives with food; feeds young; sings twice and leaves.

11:16 — Male arrives singing a 6-note song and then giving chatter-call. No feeding.

11:20 — Male comes near nest; perches quietly, then goes to feed young; sings short 3-note version of song on leaving.

11:35 — Strange new female arrives at nest! She has a lighter head and more white on the belly. Lands on different perches of nest tree; peers in nest; leaves quietly. Never called or sang.

Comment: This was exciting. This female did not call attention to herself by singing or calling. Why did she come to the nest? In other species, females sometimes dump eggs in other females' nests. Did she do this here? Were some of her young in this nest? We cannot tell.

11:36 — Male arrives with food and feeds young. Comes out of nest with fecal sac and flies 40 yards away to peach tree, where he drops it; has dropped others there. Gives chatter-call at a passing cat and flies 100 yards off.

11:44 — Male arrives with food; silent; feeds young; perches near nest. Gives "tyoot" call repeatedly. We do not see any danger in the area at first; then we see a black cat nearby. Male gives "wheet wheet wheet" call and continues "tyoot" call every 10 seconds. Flies over nearer cat; fluffs rump, showing orange; calls "tyoot" and "wheet" and chatter-call.

11:49 — Female shows up in next tree and then flies off. Male continues to give "tyoot" call every 5 seconds.

11:51 — A Cooper's Hawk flies over. Male still calling "tyoot." Female sings; arrives with food; feeds young. We note a dusky darker triangle on her tail when she is flying away.

11:52 — Male stops alarm calls. Young have continued to call since female last fed them.

Comment: Several times the alarm calls of the orioles have alerted us to what they consider danger in the area. Cooper's Hawks eat birds. Obviously these orioles are keeping a sharp eye to the sky and the ground for predators.

11:53 — Male sings and lands near female; both fly off together.

11:55 — Female arrives with food; feeds young silently; young continue to give a chattering call.
11:56 — Hear a longer song and guess that it is the male. We are right! Male arrives with food and feeds young; sings more.

Male Baltimore Oriole on pine branch.

Male Baltimore Oriole on flowering tree.

Our lunch break!

1:30 — Thunder and threatening storm in the distance; skies are gray and wind is making the nest sway in the tree.

1:51 — Male arrives with food; sings long song before we see it and we guess rightly that it is him. Feeds young; comes out of nest and ruffles breast feathers; leaves. We can now fairly reliably guess the sex of the parent by the length of the song. Male has longer song of 5–7 notes; female has song of generally 4 notes.

1:53 — Young still calling after last feeding; it is a breathy "jeejeejeejeejee."

1:54 — Young still calling.

1:57 — Female sings and then arrives with food. While perched near nest, gives "tyoot" call and chases at a crow. Comes back with food still in bill; gives two more "tyoot" calls; goes into nest and feeds young; silent on leaving.

2:01 — Female arrives with food; chatters and "tyoots"; fans tail and raises it; droops wings below body. Feeds young; then chases another female (looks like the strange female we saw earlier); continues to chase her, giving chatter-call and occasional song. Strange female has no dark throat, a grayish middle belly, and a pale crown.

2:05 — Thunder heard overhead.

2:06 — Female with food feeds young; goes to perch and preens; gives several quiet "wheet" calls. This "wheet" seems like a contact call between the pair.

2:09 — Male sings, then arrives; female flies off; male feeds young. Most food appears to be caterpillars.

2:11 — Raining slightly. We are sitting in the cargo area of our car with the back gate up, shielding us from the rain.

2:20 — Female chatters; arrives; feeds young. When she lands on the branch that the nest is attached to, the young start calling. Female leaves.

Second-year female Baltimore Oriole on branch.

2:26 — Male lands in nest tree; gives loud chatter and then flies south 100 yards.

2:28 — Male approaches nest quietly; feeds young; flies off to peach tree with fecal sac and drops it over road under the tree. We walk over to the road and see remains of 5–6 other fecal sacs.

2:38 — Male sings; comes to nest with food; feeds young; flies to perches nearby and preens; sings 3 times.

2:40 — Male goes to dogwood tree near house; hangs upside down while looking under leaves; pokes into dead curled leaves; peers all over branches. Then gives "tyoot" and chatter-calls as he lands on window ledge. We can see his reflection in the window glass. He stares at his reflection for 1 minute, gives a "tyoot" call and chatter-call, and then flies off.

Comment: When the male saw his reflection, he may have mistaken it briefly for another bird.

2:45 — Male comes to nest and feeds young; sings once; leaves.

2:46 — Male Eastern Bluebird lands in nest tree and then feeds in lawn below. A male and juvenile Red-bellied Woodpecker feed about the trunk of the nest tree together.

2:50 — Male arrives in nest tree; sings once and then leaves.

2:56 — Male arrives silently and feeds young; perches nearby.

2:57 — Female arrives with food; watches male as he chases another male Baltimore Oriole; gives a hoarse rendition of song; feeds young; leaves.

Comment: This is the first time the female has shown up in 30 minutes. We wonder where she was.

2:59 — Female arrives and feeds young quietly.

3:01 — Female arrives; feeds young; flies off with fecal sac; flies to peach tree and drops it over road where others have been dropped.

3:05 — Female arrives with food; feeds young quietly; sings once. She flies off to a nearby perch, does an action that looks like regurgitating food, and then flies back to feed young again. As female flies off, male arrives with food. One of them gives chatter-call, we can't tell which. Male feeds young and flies off quietly.

Comment: We have not read any reports of orioles regurgitating food to young at this stage of breeding. This may be a new behavioral observation.

3:09 — Male perches near nest and preens quietly; flies just above nest; sings once; flies to perch 10 yards away; sings once; leaves.

3:14 — Male is foraging among spruces nearby; flies to oaks; poops; continues foraging, often hanging upside down; looks up under leaves.

3:16 — Wind blew branches that hold nest and young started calling (maybe they thought it was the parent arriving).

3:20 — Male arrives with huge caterpillar; gives song once; leaves nest with caterpillar and starts giving repeated "tyoot" calls. We wonder what is up. Suddenly a cat walks up behind us, a new cat. Male flies over cat, giving "tyoot" call and chatter-call; flies back to nest "tyooting." Hear female sing once.

3:23 — Male continues to call at cat while female comes again and feeds young. Male calls "tyoot" every 3 seconds.

3:24 — Cat walks away from area. Male becomes quiet; flies to nest with caterpillar; feeds young; leaves.

3:26 — Northern Flicker lands within 10 feet of nest; orioles do not bother it.

3:28 — Stopped raining.

3:32 — Female arrives with food; calls "tyoot" as she approaches nest slowly; calls "tyoot" repeatedly; feeds young and flies off with fecal sac. This time fecal sac is carried in opposite direction and dropped over lawn.

3:35 — Hear "tyoot" calls from woods in back of house. Go to look and see female diving at several crows in a tree; as crows fly off, female follows and dives onto their backs, possibly hitting them, and giving chatter-calls. Crows leave area and all is quiet.

Comment: This crow-oriole interaction took place about 75 yards away from the nest. We are not sure this was the same female we were watching; we could not see its head pattern well enough. Crows can eat baby birds; this is why the oriole was chasing them.

3:39 — Male arrives in nest tree; preens; sings. Female arrives silently; feeds young. Male sings and flies off; female sings and follows.

3:42 — Male sings short song and then chases another male Baltimore Oriole to back of property. Returns to nest tree; sings; feeds young; wipes bill; sings once; flies over 200 yards to the north.
Comment: Sometimes the orioles flew off for long distances. Possibly there were feeding areas way outside their territory.

3:58 — Male arrives quietly with food; feeds young; flies off in direction of peach tree with fecal sac; drops it in the lawn. Female sings once; feeds young. Male chases another male through shrubbery.

4:01 — Female sings once; gives "tyoot" call (possibly directed at us); feeds young and leaves.

4:04 — Female arrives with food; sings once; young start calling; female feeds young and leaves.

4:07 — Female lands on nest tree; sings longer 5-note song very loudly; young call; female leaves.

4:09 — Female sings; young call; female feeds young and leaves quietly.

4:12 — Female sings once; young remain quiet; she lands on nest branch; young call; she leaves without feeding them.

4:14 — Female approaches nest quietly; feeds young; leaves. Many of the foraging trips by the parents are within 20 yards of the nest.

4:18 — Female arrives quietly; young call when she lands on nest branch; she feeds them silently; leaves.

4:22 — Female sings once, softly; feeds young and leaves.

4:23 — Female gives a very loud song once; does not approach nest.

4:25 — Female sings once again; young quiet; feeds young; brings out fecal sac and flies to peach tree; either eats fecal sac or drops it. *(Both behaviors are common.)*

4:28 — Female sings loud and long song once; feeds young and leaves.

4:30 — We leave to go home. What a great way to spend a day with the orioles!

Altamira Oriole
Icterus gularis

Why Altamira?

Altamira (the word means "high lookout") is a city in the state of Tamaulipas, Mexico. Robert Ridgeway (1850–1929), a noted ornithologist, named this bird after the area because this is where one of the first members of the species was collected. The species was originally called Lichtenstein's Oriole by a German ornithologist named Wagler, who wanted to honor his friend Martin H. Lichtenstein.

Range

The Altamira Oriole is primarily a Central American species. We see it only in the northernmost part of its range, where it ventures into the southern tip of Texas along the Rio Grande valley. Altamira Orioles are year-round residents in this region. These birds have not always been in Texas; in fact, the first verified Altamira nest was found in 1951.

The best places to see Altamira Orioles are in the Santa Ana National Wildlife Refuge, Bentsen–Rio Grande Valley State Park, and Falcon Dam, just south and west of McAllen, Texas. These areas contain tracts of the original vegetation of the Rio Grande floodplain, especially large shade trees in which the orioles like to breed.

Much of the surrounding land is cleared and used for agriculture. Part of the challenge of conserving this bird in the United States is finding ways to preserve the floodplain's native vegetation. There are presently cooperative efforts by federal, state, local, and private landholders to create a wildlife corridor along the Rio Grande from Falcon Dam to the Gulf of Mexico. These efforts deserve everyone's support.

Although Altamira Orioles are rare in the United States, it is not because their overall numbers are few. We are at the edge of their range and have dwindling breeding habitat for them; they are much more common in Mexico and farther south.

Early Breeding Behavior

Practically nothing is known about the courtship and territorial behavior of Altamira Orioles, so there is much room for the enthusiastic behavior-watcher to contribute to the general knowledge of these birds. It has been suggested that pairing occurs in the birds' first fall or spring. Altamira Orioles do not reach full adult plumage until their third year, but birds in second-year plumage can pair with other second-year birds and with full adults as well. Once paired, Altamira Orioles are believed to stay together throughout the year, although they may be more loosely associated outside the breeding season. In Mexico, they have been seen in flocks during winter.

Some observers have seen Altamira Orioles be aggressive to each other, especially in November and December; others have seen one bird chase another out of its nesting area in spring. Still others say there is no evidence of territorial behavior. In any case, if there is territoriality, it is probably only around the nest site, for the birds range up to a quarter mile from the nest to gather food for the nestlings. Nests are generally built at least 200 yards from each other.

Nest Building

In Texas, Altamira Orioles start nest building in late March. The nest is one of the most elaborately woven of any of our North American birds.

The birds choose to nest in tall trees at the tips of branches that overhang open spaces, such as across a

Altamira Oriole perched on telephone wire.

road or over the edge of an opening like a park picnic area. In one case, we saw a nest built from an overhead electric line where some Spanish moss had started to grow. The nest site averages about 25 feet above the ground and is often quite conspicuous, giving you good opportunities to watch the birds with binoculars as they build.

The female seems to do all of the building, while the male accompanies her or perches within about 50 feet; throughout nest building, the two stay in touch with short contact notes that sound like "ayk."

The nest is usually constructed over a forked branch at the tip of a limb. The birds have been observed to squeeze the prospective supporting branch with their bill, possibly testing its strength. Often a nest is started and then left unfinished, possibly because the site was ultimately deemed unsuitable in some way.

More than 200 strands of plant material are draped over the forked branches, and these are twisted and woven together. The rest of the nest is woven to and suspended from these strands. When finished, the nest is 1 1/2 to 2 feet long. The bird enters near the top and climbs down to the bottom to lay eggs and feed the young.

Materials used in the nests include Spanish moss, fine strands pulled from the edges of palmetto leaves, bark from flax, inner bark of cedar elms, pieces of vines with leaves still on them, retama leaves, horsehair, and even human-made material like the twine used to bale hay. The birds' large size and large, strong bill enable them to collect a wide range of materials.

The nest is lined with softer material such as plant down, feathers, and wool. The first nest of the season for a pair takes from 2 to 3 weeks to complete. A replacement nest, one built after a failed first nesting, may take as little as a week to build. Pairs seem to nest in the same general sites from year to year, sometimes using the same tree or even the same branch.

Certainly the position of the nest and its length help protect the orioles from predators and parasites. The supporting branches are too thin to hold most mammals and even many snakes, and the deep entrance may discourage avian predators of the eggs, such as jays, and brood parasites like the Bronzed or Brown-headed Cowbird.

Raising Young

The female lays the eggs 1 each day until there is a clutch of 3–4 eggs. The eggs are pale blue with black irregular markings. The female does all of the incubation, and the young hatch in about 14 days.

You can tell when the young have hatched, because you will see both adults approaching the nest with food. The parents make a pleasant 2-note call as they bring food. The young are fed 8–10 times each hour, and the adults may be seen leaving the nest with fecal sacs in their bills. There is no information on how long the young take to develop in the nest, but if it is like other similar-sized birds, it is probably about 12–16 days.

The young leave the nest over a period of 1–2 days, and not much is known about their behavior after they leave. They are quite quiet at this time (unlike our other young orioles), and they are probably fed by the parents for a week or two. They may even remain near the nest when the parents start a second brood, or they may move off on their own into dense lower vegetation where food is readily available.

The parents may remain in the vicinity of the nest for about a week after the young fledge. They have been noticed to be aggressive to other birds in the area during this time.

Altamira Orioles raise up to 2 broods in the United States, and breeding can continue into July.

Song and Calls

The song is a loud and long series of whistled notes on varying pitches. Pitches are similar to the range whistled by humans. Song is given by the male in spring; it is not known whether the female also sings, as is the case with many of our other orioles.

Altamira Orioles give a short single whistled note, like a single high-pitched note from the song. This may be used by the pair to keep in contact. It sounds like "ayk."

Another call is a short whistled 2-note phrase; the first is higher than the second. It sounds a little like "teekew." This is given by both male and female as they approach the nest and especially when they are feeding nestlings. The male and female also give a burst of harsh, rapid chatter during situations of alarm, such as when a potential predator nears the nest.

The Kiskadee-Kingbird Connection

Altamira Orioles are frequently observed nesting close by the nests of Great Kiskadees or Couch's Kingbirds. We saw one Altamira Oriole nest built within 15 feet of a kiskadee nest. The kiskadee was nesting between a transformer and a telephone pole, and the oriole built its nest on the telephone wire.

There is no aggression between the two species during nesting. But the kiskadee and kingbird are aggressive to Great-tailed Grackles and Bronzed and Brown-headed Cowbirds that fly into the area. Since cowbirds lay eggs in the nests of other birds, to the host's disadvantage, the oriole may be programmed to build its nest near these other species for protection from cowbird parasitism. The oriole may be similarly protected from grackles, which may eat their eggs or young.

Altamira Oriole at its long hanging nest.

Audubon's Oriole
Icterus graduacauda

Varied Habitats

The Audubon's Oriole lives in a variety of habitats, its favorite being in tall trees at the edge of open space, such as along rivers or fields. Originally, like the Altamira Oriole, it nested in trees along the Rio Grande valley. As this habitat has been converted to agricultural fields, it is fortunate that the Audubon's Oriole is able to adapt and live farther north in the much drier thorn scrub habitat.

Audubon's Oriole is primarily a Mexican species, and southern Texas is the northernmost portion of its range. It does not migrate but lives year-round within the same range. In winter it may move about and forage in small mixed flocks with other species. Pairs may remain together all year.

Audubon's Oriole perched in the thorn scrub habitat typical of parts of Texas.

Nesting

The nest of Audubon's Orioles is smaller and more cup-shaped than that of our other orioles. It is also often built well within the tree, rather than at the tips of the branches. This can make it considerably harder to find. Occasionally the nest is built within a hanging mass of Spanish moss. Mesquite is one of their favorite nesting trees in Texas.

The nest is constructed of grasses that are green at first and then dry to a yellowish color. The birds also use fibers from palmetto leaves. These are slowly pulled off the edges of the leaves; in one case an observer watched a female Audubon's Oriole take more than 7 minutes to detach one fiber.

Breeding

Breeding can begin in early April and last into June. The female lays 3–5 eggs, which are bluish with darker irregular markings. Only the female incubates, and during this time the male usually stays within 50 yards of the nest.

The pair keep in touch with each other through songs and calls. The female may even sing from the

Audubon's Oriole about to take a drink of water.

nest and the male answer. They may also give single-note calls back and forth.

The length of the incubation period is not known, but the nestling period is about 11 days. Both male and female feed the young, each making 2–3 trips per hour to the nest with food. The young are fed mostly insects, especially butterfly and moth larvae, and spiders. Both parents remove fecal sacs from the nest. In the first 2 days of nestling life they eat them; later they carry them a considerable distance from the nest. They may have up to 2 broods in a year.

The nests of Audubon's Orioles are heavily parasitized by Bronzed Cowbirds, and this may severely reduce their breeding success.

Song and Calls

Audubon's Oriole song is lower, longer, and less varied in frequency than that of the Baltimore Oriole. It consists of a series of phrases, and individual birds have consistent and recognizable patterns. An individual can vary its song by deleting phrases or by shortening the whole song. As for the quality of the song or the frequency of singing, there is no appreciable difference between the sexes.

A common call is a soft "pou-it" that seems to be a contact note between the pair as they move about and forage together. They also give a repeated high-pitched call like "ike ike ike."

Baltimore Oriole
Icterus galbula

Named After the Baseball Team?

The orange and black colors of this bird were the same as those of Lord Baltimore (1606–1675), who ruled over the colony of Maryland. This led Mark Catesby, an early ornithologist, to call it the Baltimore bird. Later it was called the Baltimore Oriole because of its similarity to the European Golden Oriole (to which it is not related). The professional baseball team in Baltimore was then named after the bird.

In the 1950s, observers discovered substantial hybridization between Bullock's Orioles and Baltimore Orioles in the Midwest. This led ornithologists to believe that the two species were really just one, and in 1983 they called them the Northern Oriole.

Recently this decision was revisited, and the Northern Oriole was deemed to be two species after all. They are now, once again, the Bullock's Oriole (living primarily in the West) and the Baltimore Oriole (living primarily in the East).

Spring Arrival

Baltimore Orioles can migrate during the day or night. Sometimes nighttime migrants continue their movement into the next morning. Also, some birds may migrate at night but continue to move slowly during the day as they feed and refuel.

In spring, Baltimore Orioles migrate in small flocks or alone. Adult males migrate first, followed by first-year males and then females a little later.

Male Baltimore Oriole on spring tree with catkins for blooms.

Two male Baltimore Orioles competing over an orange, one of their favorite foods.

They leave Central America from late February to early April, and the first arrivals in Texas and other Gulf Coast states are in late March to early April. Birds reach their northernmost breeding areas in the northern states and southern Canada by mid-May.

Baltimore Orioles migrate in spring along two routes: some fly north through Central America and Texas; others travel into the Yucatan Peninsula and then take an easterly tack across the Gulf of Mexico into Florida and Louisiana.

During migration Baltimore Orioles favor habitats much like those they use for breeding — urban parkland, woods edges, riverways, hedgerows, and suburban areas with trees.

Territorial Behavior

Adult males arrive first on their breeding territories, followed in 2–4 days by second-year males. They immediately start to sing from conspicuous perches and attempt to define and defend territories. Territories are generally small, less than an acre, and often adjacent to territories of other Baltimore Orioles. The territory serves to protect only the nest site, for the birds may leave their territory and travel 100 yards or more to feeding areas that may be shared with other Baltimore Orioles.

Defense of territory includes perching conspicuously and countersinging with a neighboring male. Intrusions by another oriole are met with the chatter-call and vigorous chases. During pauses in the chase, one or both birds may do the wing-droop display, in which their wing tips are lowered below the line of the tail. Flight-song, in which the bird flies slowly upward with deep wingbeats while singing, may also be a part of territorial advertisement.

Baltimore Orioles in the Midwest, where their range overlaps that of Bullock's Orioles, are aggressive to this species and do not let them in their territories. On the other hand, Baltimore Orioles are tolerant of Orchard Orioles in their territories.

Male Baltimore Oriole at orange.

Female Baltimore Oriole on spring blossoms.

Courtship

Females arrive about a week after the adult males, and courtship starts immediately. At first, a male may chase a female when she comes onto his territory. He may also do perch displacement, flying at the female and forcing her off her perch. At other times, when the two are perched near each other, he may hop excitedly from perch to perch and she may, in response, give the chatter-call and do wing-droop.

Later in courtship you may see the male bowing, landing in front of the female and bowing his head up and down; during this display he may have his wings spread and/or tail fanned. A melodic version of song may accompany this display. Sometimes the female responds with a precopulation display, bowing with tail fanned and raised and wings quivering, meanwhile giving a chattering call. These displays are what precedes copulation, but they do not always lead to mating.

In mating, the female leans forward, quivers her wings, and raises her tail. She may give a sound similar to food-begging by young. The male then hops onto her back and lowers his tail to make contact between their two cloacas. Following mating the male often does flight-song.

Once they are paired, the male stays close to the female to guard against her mating with other males. He is particularly vigilant during nest building, the time when most mating occurs. While she is nest building, he follows her to and from the nest as she gathers material and builds. When he sings, the female often responds with her own song or chatter-call. This may function to keep the pair in contact by sound, even if they cannot directly see each other. Upon seeing other males in his territory, he chases them out.

Even with this close watching, males often intrude on others' territories and may mate with the female. Females may meet other males while feeding off territory, and mating can occur here as well. These matings are called extra-pair copula-

Male Baltimore Oriole visiting young at last days of nestling stage.

tions, and they can result in some of the eggs in a nest having different fathers. This is a fairly common occurrence among many songbirds.

Returning to the Same Nest Site

There is a lot of variability in the nest site behavior of Baltimore Orioles. Several studies show that only 40 percent of males or females return to their breeding sites of the previous year. Those that return build nests on average about 100 yards from their previous site.

At the same time, other studies show that some orioles return to the same tree for several years in a row.

Nest Building

Usually just the female builds the nest, and she begins a few days to 2 weeks after she arrives. Nests are built 14–60 feet above the ground and placed at the tips of branches, usually among dense clusters of leaves. Trees commonly favored for nest sites include elm, cottonwood, sycamore, and aspen. Baltimore Orioles often nest along streams or roads, the nests hanging out over the open space beneath, probably for protection from predators.

The nest is beautifully constructed, 4–8 inches long, and suspended from the rim. One of the main wild sources of nesting material is old milkweed stems, which have long strong fibers that can be easily peeled off. Long fibers from the bark of grape stems are also collected. Baltimore Orioles regularly take nesting material from old oriole nests and even steal it from other active oriole nests nearby. They also collect it from debris and old clothes lying about. We have even heard of one nest made almost entirely from the mane and tail of a horse.

The lining can be feathers, grasses, wool, and dandelion or willow seed dispersal filaments. The nest is usually completed in 5–8 days but can take as much as 2 weeks to build.

Raising the Young

The female starts to lay eggs while she is adding the lining to the nest. She lays 1 egg per day until the clutch is complete — about 4–6 eggs. Eggs are usually laid in the morning and take about 30 minutes to emerge.

Eggs are pale blue to pale gray and have dark irregular blotches on them, especially at the larger end.

Incubation is done entirely by the female and takes 12–14 days. During this time the male remains nearby on the territory and occasionally may bring food to the female at the nest. If he sees any danger he may give song, tyoot-calls, or chatter-calls, to which the female may respond with song or wheet-calls from the nest. Whenever the female leaves or arrives at the nest, she gives chatter- or wheet-calls.

Until the young are about 1 week old, they are fairly quiet in the nest. After that they call when the parents approach with food. A few days before fledging they may beg more continuously, even if the parents are not there. At about this same time they may crawl to the top of the nest, or cling to the outside for moments and then crawl back in. They leave the nest after 12–13 days.

Both parents feed the young and they almost always give the chatter-call, wheet-call, or song as they approach with food. Both parents carry out fecal sacs from the nest after feeding trips.

Once the young are outside the nest, they call a great deal. At first they may stay in a nearby tree and wait for the parents to bring food, but later they follow the parents around, constantly begging. They are fed by both parents for a week or more.

In late summer, the young may join with other young and form flocks of 5–15 birds. Baltimore Orioles have only one brood.

Dealing with Cowbirds

Interestingly, Baltimore Orioles are quite effective in recognizing and protecting themselves from cowbird parasitism. They are aggressive to Brown-headed Cowbirds near the nest and will chase them away. They may also do tail-spread displays, give chatter-calls, and even peck at them.

Also, during the egg-laying period, the female Baltimore Oriole takes additional time to roost on the nest in the morning after laying her eggs. As cowbirds tend to lay eggs in the morning, the oriole's presence may discourage some cowbird activity. However, cowbirds take only 1 minute to lay an egg in a nest, while female Baltimore Orioles take about 30 minutes, so it is still easy for the cowbird to sneak in after the female oriole leaves.

Luckily, Baltimore Orioles recognize cowbird eggs in their nest almost immediately and will puncture them and then throw them out. Only about 2–3 percent of Baltimore Oriole nests are actually parasitized by cowbirds. In these cases, the young cowbird often gets most of the food and starves out the young orioles. But all in all, cowbirds do not do very well trying to parasitize Baltimore Orioles.

Fall Migration

Baltimore Orioles migrate again in early fall. They usually leave their North American breeding grounds in July until early August, and their migration reaches its peak between mid-August to mid-September. They begin to arrive on their wintering grounds in Central America in mid-August. Most migration south seems to be over land, around the Gulf of Mexico through Texas. Very few cross the Gulf in fall.

Winter Behavior

The majority of Baltimore Orioles winter in Central and northern South America. They travel about alone or in flocks of up to 15 and feed on a great deal of nectar, fruit, and some insects. They also visit feeders to sip sugar water or eat oranges, bananas, or plantains.

Small numbers of Baltimore Orioles winter in several regions of the United States. Those with the most success overwinter in the Southeast, especially Louisiana, Georgia, Florida, and the Carolinas. The few individuals that spend the winter in the Northeast may have trouble surviving the cold and are largely dependent on feeders for sustenance.

Rarely, Baltimore Orioles are seen in winter along the West Coast, in Oregon and California.

Bullock's Oriole
Icterus bullockii

Who Was Bullock?

William Bullock was an Englishman who lived from 1775 to 1840. In London he ran his own museum, which housed 3,000 species of birds, many of which he had collected, along with art from the South Seas and relics from the Napoleonic era. In addition to being a naturalist he made toys and jewelry. He also owned mines in Mexico and, while visiting his mines, added several species of birds to his collection. William Swainson, a naturalist living at about the same time, named this oriole in honor of him.

A mated pair of Bullock's Orioles taking time out.

Since the Bullock's Oriole and Baltimore Oriole hybridize in the Great Plains, these two species were thought to be just one in the 1980s — the Northern Oriole. In the mid-1990s it was decided that they were indeed two species, and so they were given back their original names.

Spring Arrival

Bullock's Orioles' winter range extends from southern Mexico south to Costa Rica. They also winter in small numbers along the West Coast, in California. In spring, they migrate north in small flocks, generally at night, and during migration they can be found in many of the same habitats in which they breed — open woodlands, river valleys, and parks.

They start to leave Mexico in March and begin to arrive in California and Arizona in mid- to late March. Bullock's Orioles flying to the Great Plains states arrive later, usually between late April and mid-May; and those flying to Canadian provinces arrive in mid-May.

Adult males are the first to arrive, followed by adult females. These in turn are followed in about 2 weeks by immatures, both males and females.

Territoriality

As soon as adult males arrive on their breeding grounds, they begin defining and defending territories. They give song from exposed perches, they chase and give rattle-calls at intruding Bullock's Orioles, and they may even fight with other males in midair.

Territories can include both a nest site and a feeding area, or just the nest site. If there is abundant food near the nest, the individual territory may be

Male Bullock's Oriole on branch.

expanded and defended. If there is little food near the nest, then just the nest site is defended and the birds go to other undefended areas to feed. These feeding areas may be over 1/2 mile from the nest and are often shared with other orioles.

Nests can be spaced out or clustered. In California there are reports of as many as 18 nests in an area of only 2 1/2 acres, but this is probably more the exception rather than the rule.

Courtship

When females first arrive on the breeding ground, they are often chased by males. This is probably not aggressive behavior; males may, in fact, be trying to keep females within their territory by chasing or almost herding them into the area. Pair formation seems to take place the same day the female arrives. Two displays that occur during this time are wing-quiver by the female, in which she assumes a horizontal posture and quivers her wings, and bowing by the male, in which he raises his bill, lowers and quivers his wings, raises and fans his tail, and bows forward. The female's wing-quiver is done during nest building and border disputes and resembles a precopulatory display. The male's bow is done toward his mate and to strange females as well.

Nest Building

Bullock's Orioles do not reuse their old nests, and their new nests are rarely in the same tree as the previous year. New nest locations average about 100 yards from where the old one was built.

Bullock's Orioles tend to breed in open woodlands, often near water, such as a stream or irrigation ditch. Stream edges with large deciduous trees, such as cottonwood, sycamore, willow, and aspen, are ideal. In other areas, they may nest in oak, mesquite, eucalyptus, box elder, or in the Northwest, even in coniferous trees such as pine, larch, or spruce. They can also nest in semiarid areas with mesquite and in trees along dry washes in mountain canyons.

The female does all of the nest building and takes about 2 weeks to complete the nest. The nest is suspended from thin twigs at the ends of a larger branch; occasionally nests are built within clusters of mistletoe growing in trees. The nest is 4–5 inches deep and has a narrow opening at the top. The female collects material of all kinds for the nest, including horsehair, string, grasses, wool, and long plant fibers. Other materials include the inner bark of willow and cottonwood, palm fibers, and strands from the stems of flax. These materials form the outside of the nest and its structure. Inside, it is lined with downy materials such as the dispersal fluff from the seeds of cottonwood or willow and even feathers.

As with many other orioles, the nest may be in the same tree with breeding Western or Eastern Kingbirds and, in Texas, near the nests of Scissor-tailed Flycatchers. Nesting near these aggressive and alert birds may aid Bullock's Orioles in defending their nest against predators and cowbird parasitism.

Male Bullock's Oriole feeding nestlings.

Breeding

The female lays 4–5 eggs that are pale bluish to whitish with dark speckling, especially heavy at the larger end. If the male of the pair is an immature bird, the size of the clutch tends to be smaller. The female does all of the incubation, and this lasts for 11 days. During this time, the male stays near the nest, and if any potential predator comes near, both male and female may dive at it, calling and chasing it out of the area.

Both male and female feed the nestlings. It takes 14 days before the young are old enough to leave the nest. The young may stay in or near the nest tree for several days after fledging, and the parents continue to feed them for several weeks.

After a few days, the family moves away from the nest area and may join with other Bullock's Oriole families. These groups on occasion can grow as large as 100 birds.

Bullock's Orioles usually live 3–4 years; there is a record of one living 8 years. They have only 1 brood per year.

Fall Departure

Bullock's Orioles begin to leave their breeding areas long before fall. In California, they may start leaving by mid- to late July, at which time adult males, which migrate first, are hard to find. In more northern areas, they rarely stay past late August to mid-September. They must take their time moving south, for they do not arrive on their wintering grounds until October or early November.

Songs

The song of the Bullock's Oriole is less musical than those of our other orioles. Rather than being composed of a series of whistles, it is a string of harsher notes, reminiscent of a Gray Catbird's song. Both male and female Bullock's Orioles sing. Their songs are similar, but the endings may vary, with the female's being slightly harsher.

Males sing as soon as they arrive on their breeding territories, and their notes seem to function as advertisement, defense, and mate attraction. Females often sing while they are defending the territory.

Male Bullock's Oriole on stump.

A rapid chatter-call is used in times of alarm and given at potential predators. Single call notes include a short "kip" and a more drawn-out "keeek." The function of these calls is not known for sure, but they may serve as contact notes.

What They Eat in the Wild

The main insect prey of Bullock's Orioles is often the caterpillars of moths and butterflies gleaned from tree and shrub leaves at heights of about 5–35 feet. They can eat a great many tent caterpillars in spring. Their other main insect prey is grasshoppers, which they catch on or near the ground. Also of interest are beetles, bugs, ants, and even bees (they remove the stinger before eating). Occasionally, Bullock's Orioles may catch butterflies, dragonflies, and other insects in the air like a flycatcher.

Nectar is gathered from flowers, especially in winter and spring. They gather nectar from agave, eucalyptus, coral bean, ocotillo, red-hot poker, and other flowers. They also come to hummingbird or oriole sugar water feeders in backyards.

Particularly during summer, Bullock's Orioles feed on fruit of all kinds, including blackberries and raspberries, elderberries, cherries, hawthorn berries, and apricots. They sometimes eat larger fruits by "gaping" — poking their closed beak into the fruit and opening it — then lapping up the juices with their tongue.

Hooded Oriole
Icterus cucullatus

Spring Arrival

Hooded Orioles tend to migrate in small flocks in spring. Males arrive slightly ahead of females, and appear in Texas by mid-March. They arrive in mid- to late March in New Mexico and Arizona and mid-March to early April in California.

Since the early 1900s, the Hooded Oriole has been expanding its range in California. Its range has spread north of San Francisco nearly to the border of Oregon, probably as a result of urbanization and the accompanying plantings in parks and backyards.

Although its range includes the Southwest, it is not found in the drier areas of yuccas and junipers, which is the typical habitat of the Scott's Oriole.

In the Southwest, the Hooded Oriole is usually found close to water. Traditionally it probably lived in the cottonwoods and mesquite bordering streams and rivers. Then, as has happened in northern California, with urban settlement it has been able to feed and nest in the lush plantings around suburban houses and in city parks and gardens. It shares some of this habitat with the Bullock's Oriole but is generally quieter and more secretive than that species.

Female Hooded Oriole at hummingbird feeder.

Male Hooded Oriole on stump.

Geographic Variation

The Hooded Oriole's size and color vary across the United States. These variations have been divided into three subspecies. The largest and yellowest subspecies is called *nelsoni (Icterus cucullatus nelsoni)*. It breeds from California to western Texas; it has the longest bill and very little orange in its adult plumage.

The second species, *cucullatus (I. c. cucullatus)*, is medium-sized. The adult female is tinged with orange, while the adult male has an orange head. This subspecies breeds in south-central Texas.

The subspecies *sennetti (I. c. sennetti)* breeds in

southern Texas. It is the smallest of the three and the most deep orange in plumage.

The Palm-leaf Oriole

In southern California, the Hooded Oriole builds its nest most often within the fronds of palms or the leaves of palmettos. Of all the palms, the Washington palm *(Washingtonia filifera)* is by far its favorite nest tree; in addition, most of the nests in southern California are also made of the fibers from Washington palm. Because of this the Hooded Oriole is sometimes called the Palm-leaf Oriole.

The birds secure the nest to the underside of the leaves by poking holes through the leaves and weaving fibers through the holes. Often the weaving has the effect of drawing the supporting leaves together and giving the nest added protection from the elements and predators. Nests can be from 10 to 45 feet above the ground. Sometimes the nests are also suspended under the large leaves of banana trees.

In Arizona, New Mexico, and Texas, the Hooded Oriole is more likely to build its nest in a variety of trees, and will even occasionally use the base of mistletoe clusters growing on cottonwoods or mesquite trees. In these regions, the nests are often built almost entirely of thin, tough grasses, collected when they are green. The grasses tend to remain green and camouflage the nest. Some nests may be made of yucca fibers, and their beige color then makes the nest more conspicuous.

A new nest is built for each of the 2–3 broods. The male accompanies the female on her trips to and from the nest as she does all of the building. She works fast and can finish in 3–4 days. Occasionally, oriole nests are used by House Finches when the orioles have left; sometimes the finches take over even before the orioles have nested.

Breeding

Courtship among Hooded Orioles has not been well studied. Early stages include chases of the female by the male. The male sometimes does a bowing display while perched near the female. He can also do a bill-up display in front of the female while singing softly at the same time. The function of these displays is unknown.

The female lays 3–5 eggs, 1 each day. They are pale buff or bluish white with darker splotches that are denser at the larger end of the egg. Incubation is done only by the female and lasts 12–14 days. The nestlings are fed by regurgitation for the first 4–5 days; after that they are brought whole insects. They are fed by both parents and can leave the nest in

Female Hooded Oriole at nest.

Male Hooded Oriole bringing a fledgling to a sugar water feeder.

about 2 weeks. In summer, young from early broods may stay together and move about as a small flock. Two to three broods are raised, and breeding occurs from April into August.

The Hooded Oriole is parasitized fairly heavily by both Bronzed and Brown-headed Cowbirds.

Feeding

Hooded Orioles feed on insects in a variety of ways: hopping after grasshoppers on the ground, gleaning caterpillars from under leaves, and searching bark crevices for smaller insects. Often they walk along branches rather than fly from spot to spot. Hooded Orioles also often hang upside down as they look for insects and spiders in crevices. This gives them an advantage over species of birds that cannot do this, for they can see into more nooks and crannies for potential food.

In natural habitats, they tend to feed in deciduous trees and shrubs along streams and rivers. Besides insects, they also eat fruits such as berries, cherries, and loquats, and nectar from agave, aloe, hibiscus, and lily. They may peck through the base of large flowers to get at the nectar as they perch on the stems. They may even poke into unopened buds.

Hooded Orioles also come to sugar water feeders of all kinds.

Song

Male Hooded Orioles may sing from the tops of trees, and their song is warbling in quality and generally quieter than that of other orioles. Hooded Orioles have a chatter-call much like that of other orioles, but it is a little softer. The birds commonly give a soft chirp at regular intervals.

Summer's End

Most Hooded Orioles have left the northern portions of their breeding range by the end of August, and southern areas by early September. A few birds may overwinter in southern California and southeastern Arizona, often staying close to sugar water feeders.

Orchard Oriole
Icterus spurius

Spring Migration

Orchard Orioles start migration north in early March, when they leave the southernmost portion of their breeding range in Colombia and Venezuela. They pass through Panama by mid-March and are most abundant in Veracruz, Mexico, from late March to early April.

The birds commonly take two different routes north, the paths diverging when they reach Guate-

Second-year male Orchard Oriole.

mala. Some head east out to the tip of the Yucatan Peninsula and then fly across the Gulf of Mexico to locations along the U.S. coast from Louisiana to Florida. Others stay over land and continue north along the eastern edge of Mexico and Texas. This differs from fall migration, when all Orchard Orioles seem to travel south along the Gulf Coast through Texas and none across the Gulf.

The first Orchard Orioles generally arrive in Texas in late March and early April and the cross-Gulf migrants arrive at about the same time in Florida and Louisiana.

The birds are nocturnal migrants and move north as a broad front, but they are more concentrated along the Mississippi River valley than in other areas. On average they arrive in the northernmost portion of their breeding range, such as Vermont and the Dakotas, about mid-May. The earliest arrivals in these areas appear in late April.

Expanding Range

Within the last thirty to forty years, the Orchard Oriole has been expanding its breeding range in several directions — north into Manitoba, west into Colorado, and south into Florida. However, this range expansion does not seem to be due to a healthy population. The numbers of Orchard Orioles have been dropping regularly, most in the central states and less so in the eastern states.

Early Breeding Behavior

Second-year and adult males arrive on the breeding grounds at almost the same time. Right away you may see chases between males; it is not clear whether these are to defend nest sites or defend foraging areas. Females arrive a little later,

Male Orchard Oriole on branch.

and there are then chases between males and females.

Look for several visual displays during the first few weeks — the bow, seesaw, wing-flutter, and flight display. The first three take place on perches. In the bow, the bird tilts its body forward while facing another bird; this exposes the colors of the back, rump, and tail to the other bird. In the seesaw, the bird rocks forward and back. And in wing-flutter, the wings are partly opened and fluttered while the bird gives a high trill. A fourth display takes place in flight. Done only by males, this is a slow, stalling flight with the bird raising and lowering its tail.

Both males and females in their second year can breed. Males at this time are not in their full adult plumage. Second-year males are often the ones to try breeding in marginal habitats or at the edges of the species' range. For example, most of the males trying to breed in Vermont are second-year males.

Nest Building

Orchard Orioles build one of the shallowest nests of all our North American Orioles. Their nests are about 4 inches wide and only about 3 inches high.

The nest is built about 10–20 feet above the ground but can be as low as 4 feet and as high as 60 feet. It is suspended from forked twigs at the end of a branch, often among the tree's leaves, making it quite camouflaged. Occasionally nests are placed in the upright fork of branches. Along the Gulf Coast, nests are sometimes built in tall grasses called phragmites, and in the South, they can be found in clumps of Spanish moss.

One way to recognize an Orchard Oriole nest is by its yellow color. This comes from the use of grasses in construction. They are green when first collected and used in building but then dry to a golden yellow. Orchard Orioles use strands of grass up to 30 inches long, taken from a variety of species, depending on what is available in the area. They also use other long fibers, such as those from yuccas. The nests are lined with soft downy fibers such as wool, yarn, or feathers, or the dispersal filaments from the seeds of cattail and willow.

The nest is built almost exclusively by the female and takes 3–6 days to complete.

Coloniality

There have been many reports of Orchard Orioles nesting near each other. In one case, someone observed 18 nests of Orchard Orioles all in one tree. In another case, 114 nests were discovered on 7 acres.

Nonetheless, it is perhaps more common to find their nests spaced out. The factors causing this species to choose colonial or solitary nesting are not know. Coloniality is perhaps more likely to occur where the birds are abundant and food resources are ample, such as in the Gulf Coast states.

In either case, Orchard Orioles are not particularly territorial, although they can be aggressive just prior to egg laying. This is the period when mating also occurs, and males may be guarding their mates from mating with other males.

As with some other oriole species, Orchard Orioles often nest near kingbirds, in this case usually Eastern Kingbirds, and gain some protection from predators due to the kingbird's aggressiveness toward potentially dangerous intruders.

Raising the Young

The female lays an average of 4–5 eggs, which have a pale blue or gray background with darker blotches mostly on the larger end. Incubation starts after the final egg is laid and lasts 12–14 days. The female does all of the incubation, and during this time the male often comes to the nest to bring her food. She also takes breaks from the nest to preen and feed herself.

Once the young hatch, both parents feed them, making trips as often as 12 times per hour. Some observers have seen second-year males attending the nests of older males, helping them feed the nestlings. During the nestling stage, both parents vigorously defend the nest against other birds that might prey on the young, such as jays, crows, or grackles. The young fledge at about 11–14 days and then may remain in the area of the nest with the parents for an additional week before moving with the whole family to another location where food is more plentiful. Sometimes at this stage the parents divide up the young, and each parent takes care of certain individuals in the brood.

In July and August, various families of Orchard

Male Orchard Oriole feeding young a caterpillar.

Female Orchard Oriole looking for food in spring.

Orioles may join together and roam about in search of food. At this time they may feed on berries, grasshoppers, and other foods that are abundant.

Fall Migration

Orchard Orioles are one of the earliest songbirds to migrate. Second-year and adult males start migrating south first, some as soon as late July. At the same time, fledglings and females join together into flocks of up to 30 birds. They feed and move about together for another 4–6 weeks before flying south to join the males.

The southward migration is believed to be solely around the Gulf of Mexico, because after about mid-July very few Orchard Orioles are seen in Florida. They sometimes arrive in Central America as early as July 20.

Winter Behavior in South and Central America

Unlike most of our other orioles, Orchard Orioles migrate south before undergoing their complete pre-basic molt. Thus, they arrive on their wintering grounds in worn plumage.

On their wintering grounds, they inhabit mostly lowland areas at the edge of dense vegetation or in cut-over forests or cultivated fields. They move about in flocks, often feeding on nectar. Sometimes they visit banana plantations, where they hang upside down while feeding on nectar from the banana flowers.

They often form roosts each night in tall grasses, dense vines, or small trees and may be joined by other orioles, other migrants, and resident finches. They also may be heard singing on the wintering grounds, mostly just after they arrive in August and September and then again just before they leave in March.

Scott's Oriole
Icterus parisorum

Naming Competition

Winfield Scott (1786 to 1866) was an American commander in the Mexican War. During the war, one of his lieutenants, a naturalist named Darius Nash Couch, believed that Scott had discovered a new species of oriole. Couch later named the oriole for his commander, calling it *Icterus scottii*, but it turned out that Charles Bonaparte had already named this species *Icterus parisorum*, after brothers named Paris who dealt in natural history specimens.

As is the scientific custom, the scientific name reverted to the first given name, *Icterus parisorum*, but interestingly, the common name has remained Scott's Oriole.

Who Breeds

Studies of Scott's Orioles have shown that almost all adult birds breed in any given year. It has also been shown that all second-year females breed with adult males, if there are enough to go around. This leaves the second-year males out in the cold, so to speak. In general, second-year males only breed

Second-year male Scott's Oriole.

Male Scott's Oriole on stump.

when there are not enough adult males available. These same studies have also shown that in most years the total population consists of more males than females.

The excess males that do not breed are sometimes called "floaters." Some of them may function as replacements, mating with females that lose a male during the breeding season.

Nest Building

The Scott's Oriole is known for choosing semiarid areas in which to breed. In these locations its preferred nesting plant is treelike yuccas. The nest is usually built within the clusters of leaves at the top of the plant, woven among the living leaves that hang down. Some species of yucca in which they regularly build nests include soap tree *(Yucca elata),* Thompson's yucca, *(Y. rostrata),* and Joshua tree.

At higher elevations, or in areas where there is slightly more water, they may use sycamore, oak, pine, and candlewood trees. Nests are 4–60 feet above the ground, most commonly 10–20 feet high.

The nest is less pensile (hanging) than most other oriole nests, being about 3 1/2 inches wide and about 4 inches deep. It is woven around branches and sometimes even incorporates leaves into the body of the nest. The nest is constructed of fibers often peeled from other species of yucca, such as Spanish dagger *(Y. treculeana)* and giant dagger *(Y. faxoniana).* Also in the external structure are fine grasses taken when they are green. The interior of the nest is composed of finer grasses and lined with cottony dispersal fibers from various plants' seeds. The nests are usually well concealed.

While the female does all of the building, the male usually perches nearby and may accompany the female on her trips to get nesting material. After 6–10 days the nest is built; then the pair leave the nest for 2–4 days before the female returns to lay the first egg.

Territories and Pairing

Scott's Orioles usually nest quite far apart. The closest nests in one study were between 150 and 200 yards apart. The distance does not seem to be the result of territorial defense, however, for there are very few interactions between males or females that look like aggression. The pairs just seem to space themselves evenly across the landscape, and aggression occurs only when a strange oriole approaches another nest too closely.

Pairs or individuals leaving their nest areas to feed elsewhere on insects or nectar from flowers may fly over other nest sites with no reaction from the owners.

In the majority of cases, males and females find new mates each year. Males tend to return closer to where they bred in the previous year than females, but birds usually build new nests several hundred yards from where their old one was built.

Breeding

The eggs are pale bluish white and have dark markings all over them, the markings sometimes concentrated at the larger end. The female lays from 1 to 5 eggs but the most common clutch size is 3.

Evidence of hatching times shows that the young usually hatch over a 2-day period. In most cases, where there are 3-egg clutches, 2 of the eggs hatch within hours of each other and the third hatches 12 or more hours later. The female probably does not start incubating until after the second egg is laid. Total incubation time is about 12–13 days. The male may bring food to the female during the later stages of incubation, but he usually just perches near the nest.

About 12 days after hatching, the young leave the nest and are fed by both parents. The family leaves the nesting area about a day after the young fledge.

The female starts a second brood 2–3 weeks after the young fledge from the first nest. Sometimes

Male and female Scott's Orioles feeding at an orange nailed to a tree.

Male Scott's Oriole checking on its nest.

Scott's Orioles have a third brood, and this is usually started as soon as 1 week after the young from the second brood have fledged. While the female starts second and third clutches, the male continues to feed the fledglings from the previous clutch until they are independent.

The pair almost always stay together for all nesting attempts in a given season, and the female builds a new nest for each brood, usually in a new location.

Spring Arrival, Fall Departure, and Wintering

In spring, adult male Scott's Orioles are the first to arrive. They usually appear in southern California and southern Arizona in mid-March. They are followed by the adult females and soon after by second-year males and females. Scott's Orioles often migrate north in small flocks of 6–12 birds.

By mid-August the birds start to leave their breeding grounds and are less frequently heard singing. By mid-September they have pretty much left the United States. A few Scott's Orioles may overwinter in southeastern Arizona.

Predators and Parasites

Scott's Orioles can be destroyed by a variety of predators. Among mammals, mice, rats, and raccoons eat the eggs, the larger mammals often destroying the nest as they look for eggs and young. Snakes, such as the rat snakes, may take the eggs or young without disturbing the nesting material.

Among the birds who disturb Scott's Orioles, House Finches sometimes take over the nests, and screech-owls and Great Horned Owls can eat the nestlings.

The Bronzed Cowbird occasionally lays eggs in the nests of Scott's Orioles, and in these cases the orioles often abandon the nest and rebuild elsewhere.

Food

Scott's Orioles eat a variety of fruits, insects, and nectar. They are known to frequent orchards, if they are nearby, and eat apricots, figs, and peaches. They may also eat the fruits of cactus.

In spring and summer, these orioles often feed on nectar and insects from opuntia, agave, and yucca. The insects they eat include beetles, grasshoppers, caterpillars, and butterflies.

Spot-breasted Oriole
Icterus pectoralis

An Introduced Oriole

No one is quite sure when or how the Spot-breasted Oriole was introduced into southern Florida. It was first seen in 1949 in Coconut Grove, and may have originally been brought from elsewhere in captivity, since this species is sometimes kept as a caged bird. The population expanded for the next twenty-five years and then started to decrease dramatically. It now seems to have stabilized. Cold winters seem to be hard on Spot-breasted Orioles and may reduce their numbers.

Its native range is from the Pacific lowlands in southwestern Mexico to central Costa Rica and locally on the Caribbean slope of Guatemala and Honduras. Its native habitat is semiarid brush and the edges of tropical hardwood forests.

In Florida the Spot-breasted Oriole lives in the southeastern portion of the coast, from Homestead in the south to just north of Jupiter. In its new home it lives in heavily planted suburban backyards with tall trees, where it feeds on small fruits, insects, and nectar. It is known to break off hibiscus flowers to get at the nectar.

Behavior

The Spot-breasted Oriole starts breeding in April, and in summer it is the only oriole seen in southeastern Florida. During breeding it may sit on exposed perches and sing its loud and continuous series of flutelike whistles. Its nest is suspended, like that of other orioles, and made of grasses and palm fibers.

It lays 3–5 eggs that are pale bluish with darker markings. Timing of incubation and fledgling stages are not yet known. It does seem to have at least 2 broods per year. After breeding, the birds tend to spend the winter in small flocks.

Several Spot-breasted Orioles have been banded, and one was recaptured over seven years later, showing that they can live at least that long.

The birds are residents both in Florida and in their native range and do not migrate.

Plumage

The adult male and adult female look essentially the same, although the female may not be as brightly orange. As adults, they lack a white bar on their greater coverts and have strong white edging on their secondaries. The first- and second-year birds are slightly more muted and may not have spots on their breast.

Spot-breasted Oriole.

Streak-backed Oriole
Icterus pustulatus

A Rare Visitor

The Streak-backed Oriole lives primarily from northwestern Mexico south to Costa Rica, where it inhabits brushy thorn forests and wooded stream-sides.

In the past, these orioles have been seen in the United States only in southeastern Arizona and southern California, at the extreme northern edge of their range, usually in fall and winter. This may have occurred because the northwestern Mexico populations of this species are partially migratory and may have strayed off course into the United States.

In the last few years, however, several pairs of Streak-backed Orioles have stayed through summer in southeastern Arizona and are actually breeding.

Behavior

The sounds of this species include a scolding rattle, a soft "wheet" call, and a song that is composed of a short series of notes like "chip chip cheet cher." In its native habitat it builds a long hanging nest, often placed in acacia trees. Besides long natural fibers, human-made cloth or twine may be incorporated into their nests. Sometimes several birds may build nests in the same tree.

Plumage

The Spot-breasted Oriole was formerly called the Scarlet-headed Oriole in reference to the bright orange-red head of the adult male; the deep red seems to take several years to develop. The adult female is similar, but her colors are more muted. Both have black on the throat and face and streaking on the back. The second-year bird is similar to the female but has no black on the face and throat and little or no streaking on the back; its body is more greenish or orangish yellow than the brighter orange of the adults. In the second year, males and females look similar.

Female Streak-backed Oriole at nest.

Resources

Oriole Feeder Manufacturers

Nature Products Incorporated
P. O. Box 277
West Kingston, RI 02892
Web site: www.natureproducts.com
E-mail: natureproducts@riconnect.com

Opus Incorporated
P. O. Box 525
Bellingham, MA 02019
Web site: www.opususa.com

Perky Pet Products
2201 South Wabash Street
Denver, CO 80231
Web site: www.perky-pet.com

Mealworms (Mail Order Sources)

Grubco
Hamilton, OH
1-800-222-3563

Nature's Rainbow Company
Ross, OH
1-800-688-6972

Bird Magazines

Birder's World
P. O. Box 1612
Waukesha, WI 53187-1612
1-800-446-5489
Web site: www.birdersworld.com
E-mail: customerservice@kalmbach.com

Bird Watcher's Digest
P. O. Box 110
Marietta, OH 45750
1-800-879-2473

WildBird
P. O. Box 6040
Mission Viejo, CA 92690
1-800-365-4421
E-mail: wildbird@fancypub.com

Societies

Cornell Laboratory of Ornithology
Project FeederWatch
159 Sapsucker Woods Road
Ithaca, NY 14850
Web site: www.birds.cornell.edu
E-mail: cornellbirds@cornell.edu

National Bird-feeding Society
P. O. Box 23
Northbrook, IL 60065-0023
Phone: 847-272-0135
Fax: 847-498-4092
E-mail: birdseye1@aol.com

Books

Bent, A. C. 1958. *Life Histories of North American Blackbirds, Orioles, Tanagers, and Allies.* New York: Dover.

Orians, Gordon. 1985. *Blackbirds of the Americas.* Seattle: University of Washington.

Poole, Alan, and Frank Gill, eds. 1966. *Birds of North America.* Philadelphia: Academy of Natural Sciences.